JARED DANIEL FAGEN

THE ANIMAL OF EXISTENCE

BSE

ISBN: 979-8-9860369-0-8

BSE Books are distributed by
 Small Press Distribution
 1341 Seventh Street
 Berkeley, CA 94710
 orders@spdbooks.org | www.spdbooks.org
 1-800-869-7553

BSE Books can also be purchased at
www.blacksquareeditions.org and www.hyperallergic.com

Contributions to BSE can be made to
 Off the Park Press, Inc.
 976 Kensington Ave.
 Plainfield, NJ 07060

(Please make checks payable to Off the Park Press, Inc.)

To contact the Press please write:
 Black Square Editions
 1200 Broadway, Suite 3C
 New York, NY 10001

An independent subsidiary of Off the Park Press, Inc.
Member of CLMP.

Publisher: John Yau
Editors: Ronna Lebo and Boni Joi
Design & composition: Shanna Compton

Cover art: Christine Shan Shan Hou, *dream triptych* (detail), 2021. Collage on
paper. By permission of the artist.

Praise for *The Animal of Existence*

Language is a dangerous, burning, woods. "What's at stake is thus far what survives the inferno." And in those hot thickets, *The Animal of Existence* by Jared Daniel Fagen is itself a complex animal—crouching, questioning, restless, at times stalking the edges of consciousness, at times wild of mouth, with an electric, charged bite. It offers a series of poetic prose texts, hybrid in their inventive logics of narrative and syntax, each piece carrying distinct music and texture. "I am walled and rung alive by your love, your love annihilated me from the territory of circumferences, of your retina." This book powerfully wrangles alienation and identity, as well as grief, hard feelings, and "the mourning dusk of us." The angles are vividly torqued, and they touch the delicate nerves. "Say I a wound instead." —**Sawako Nakayasu**

How does one draw lingual heat from the timeless dark in which perception rests? By preparing one's self for alteration as a sign-in-oneself. Only poets know what I mean. For everyone else, we'll say that "to crave contact ridicules the tundra within." The other issue is one of exchanging gods for visions in katabasis: in the midnight of the consciousness of the "face returning, featureless, not belonging in the throngs or torrent, but the throes," exists an animal preserved by the torture of its persistent reification, the words it (with)holds panic to restore the significance of this ultimate nothingness, yet when they do not, cannot, when it does not, when the end is found to be endless, the Creative Silence drags up its sea of possibilities and sews it to the night, with image as the debt of the animal's awareness, revolving toward the miraculous, the moment clouded by "apostrophe, molten," cognitive with dizziness from the temporary light that slides over us by day. In these epistemological bulletins, Fagen drives "the heirloom of abhorrence," or the apple of articulate injury, from "hallucination" and "secludedness, riposting the iris," and so on and so forth. "How much time has passed?" —**Carlos Lara**

for ELF
Bb
Cassie
& Beefy

Contents

prelude to antonym

*From the "not yet" to the "no longer"—this is
the path of what we call the writer . . .*

—Maurice Blanchot

RATHER/INSOMN

Desperate to write I could not write. Unable, he had begun: the awful insomnia of my gathered wrote. I return to attempt him once more, for the last forgery, to form the formerly refused entrances and cursive distance.

To write I pray. To pray only prolongs the posture of my pleading.

I write the Promethean wound. I write without bloom. I write for him merely to be no more than meagerly enough. I write not to reflect but, rather, to reverberate: to capture him stateless in the rapture of splitting daybreaks.

Writing the dawns to apprehend his origin. The writing that bastardized a life withheld but with anguish recorded without reason. Writing with little care for accuracy, against a nightgown of starlight, I reminisce him like this: requiting the injury of having been articulated.

I learned the labor of writing by replicating him, so close to impotence. Gathering, gnawing, hissing, I've kept vigil. I know I should turn and look away, but I've often gone on in disobedience of what I know.

The horror is I realize him.

Before language there were the screams, after words there was growing into silence. In the interim I reinvent his memories in which I am surrogate: the muffled source, what later he would not become, detest being, finally repudiating me.

There's sleep and there's what we've not been allowed.

Wide-eyed to his torments, heavy lids lifted my pen. I work late in the abandoned study, wherein memory makes a fault line across my enclosure. All I bid that remains of him, the pages tarred and teared ridges of paltry prayered and wondered words. I write with and beside such wonder: is the silence of this room willful?

For him I've grieved and gone hungry, learned to lie and to loathe. Seen, saw wrongfully. What does the profile of a mountain resemble from where I stand, other than itself looking away from me? I have known cliffs, I summon him to the precipice, and only at the summit, together teasing the plunge, do we become familiar. Like he with the glacial contours of my tongue: sheer and vertiginously sharp.

I reckon these words that have amassed him with waning inquiry, a meticulous depravity, hoping there is some part of him left to surrender me. That each pitiable word within what little means at my disposal says everything frenzied of blushing untended meadows. Are they plenty enough bereft? Dare I amend?

We risk the climb and still not heard.

Now I wince skimming with impatience, distraught even, turning leaves absentmindedly and too tortured. I am at fault whom dared to look back, to bear him begun, to vindicate that which cannot be completed. Of him I am antonym: reduced, resisting and barely, our shared annihilation. For him it will be as it is for me: the unfortunate unfinishable happening.

I'm writing his prehistory into epitaphs. I'm always writing the epitaphs, he had to start somewhere. At the beginning and the end we are wicked animals, our howls indifferent toward extinction and self-directed malice. On the cusp of being born I write his language into my despicable inheritance. The words already come out the same: the heirloom of abhorrence.

We've come to this: wind. Write: obliterate sustenance.

I read him famished for so long the pains of me deplete I can no longer lament. It would seem I like where this is going, is it too late to turn back? To flee? No, I want with length almond eyes and oblique canoes to set fire to, to be capsized and drowned in, a longevity by which to perpetually perish. I'm lying again, to myself, for him: the writing suffers us now more acutely in the temples, within where I reperform his documentary.

I return to him rather than, almost, since those he's lost touch with refuse to reappear without my interference. It hurts having seen the parts of him stayed with me, and those parts without remaining infliction. What's worse is I give narration to the hymn: I step into a blizzard that sirens. These words, they rewrite the lacerations.

Into the vice I toss, into the infirmary he abides my hostility. I don't want to. But the infinitive guilt of barely *to be* is the old gauze I bleed through.

I write him, the aforementioned. There are things I read now that he could not possibly remember: the etymologies of his name ("the top," "a stone"), by whom he was orphaned (hereby certified), the appraisal of his development (in the third-person singular). I know these things both deterred and unwittingly dredged, to claim a purity of essence.

Betrothed to a neutral echo, as I violate him with folded hands.

The cutaway angle trains on testimonies of his having been: photocopied papers, illegible notes along the margins, amounts partially enclosed by hastily drawn circles, their curves that do not complete themselves. I resume him reduced, so precious little, I suppose to purge the hurt, but piss and vinegar stir within.

His emptiness gained, for me it's feasible, to write the spreading hand of sundials. The acute accrues into biting futures. They gather, they tremble, with a beige momentum that yet waxes sleepless.

Here it is he was begun: the providence of reproof. Here it is he became: the insomnia of a page.

I return sudden but with deliberation, defamation, the foresaw. A thought so sudden is sentencing. The writing, it is never complete. I compose, compile, keep the deficient, give him another door to shut, another ravenous handful. He scaled, he tumbled, the innocent act of improvisation. Like when he was young and adjusting, praying to anything porcelain.

The lens kept out of focus, the script equally as reticent as he remains. What's at stake is thus far what survives the inferno. Rather an approximation of flames, impossible recoveries. I am he that he will become: the gesture of a grasp gripping air and collapsing into the maternal arms of combustible nitrate.

How is it symmetry formed, how is it we are of so much squalor, still? There is a thing such as force, there is force from somewhere off. The force is felt in the writing, my obstinate effort to recuperate him by reciting what I've come to but am still unable to say. Because he is powerless and I aghast and ugly, amiss in the nature of looking.

I'm watching him act in a foreign film, monstrously rising from the soil. There are so many theaters in which lights were insufficiently dim. There are so many screens on which he'd danced unknowingly. He is that refugee of my self and long ago mountains. I force again the first impression.

I make revisions then refuse to revise. I can't keep this going so I tear out, with remorse for failed dissections. To write is to blow dandelion kisses in the wind to absent lips, stumbling in the breeze with their petty sidewalk swagger. Rather I have staggered, stabbing sidewalks with my wanderlust.

Incapable of falling asleep to the syncopation of steps, I've kept him juvenile. A child pulling the chains of a tire swing to gain the velocity I will lose for us, rather watching me lose it, watching my engulfment, as I hope inscribing him might assist the futile thaw.

Can a prelude be perpetual? Can a preface wear away, rather than give way? Dare I write in memoriam of a name that lived in his place? I don't know the proper pronunciation, never heard it spoke toward him. Now it's mine: I write to timidly wrap it into a whisper, into purses brimming with twigs and scorpion grass.

Neither these words I never knew how to say, still. I count how many words I had written of which, still, I am afraid. The fear, however, is not the force: it is how to say I read him back to myself and resolve I'm afraid of death. Rather at last apologetic for dying here, wrote and whimpering.

My death will be his origin, his origin will be a pacemaker of days. The frame is lacunae. The gap: an emptiness and an opening.

He had begun with the miracle that is waking. Begun that day that will be, when he's not supposed to. Begun frightened that day is near, when I'm supposed to. He was beginning to, against deictic days that should be.

He had begun a branch that became a toothpick, a nail file, the scope of a rifle, something to splice or shave. He began wearing pleated pants poured over chafed winter roots, scared of scorched frontiers.

He had begun uncertain whens with an obelisk in his chest, drawn blinds across its dunes. Begun a pyramidion plume of light, a virgin of the sky, a den of rain. He was beginning whens as an evacuation, emptying epithets of their creased petals, pulling taught the crutch of my wing. An albatross blowing dust to vestige me.

But to end the whens I must unhow. To end with the interencounter, a craned-neck *dérive*, plunged and plummeting. A prefix complicates my boundary crossing, peripheral days of sand, a finished wish to start over.

I return from a long absence, I return abundantly to the betrayal of words. When I was gone, memory restored and verified our lack. In the interlude I heard echoes weeping like a cataract, cascading into dark apertures.

Now I dig ravishing cavities, pace uprooted dirt, pull splinters from my persons. Dispersed in the darkness, journeying past through the dearth, I beat memory into his appearance. I drink it all, atoms and suns, and burn speechless in the swallows. To look back, to die and refute time, joins us to the incandescent avalanche.

I write him: begins.

The mourning dusk of us.

absent of life

With these coarsened traits making me invisible
Spoiled still more under the lenses of the rain
I hate myself even in the rooms
The guillotines lacerated at night

—Michel Deguy

ASUNDER

Forgive my trespasses, at first they were innocent. But for long, for much too long, you have been asunder. I cannot court sleep again with you so torn. Alas I can no longer love, wearily, without you unbroken, to recite for me, deliriously like you used to, passages from *On the Heights of Despair*, lines from *Lightduress* and *La Fin du monde*. When I loved every severed piece of you, if only not *to forget that life is death's prisoner*. You defiled me so dexterous, so entirely to shreds you said love was proved by the words I spoke from you, through me, yours. Back then we mealed on bread and hot sauce, remember? Remember me at my hollowest? Rationing three slices of rye per day, twice as much that Easter, when you painted eggs into the busts of Roman emperors. Now years gone by since descent brought me to words. Poverty of words. There you were, I was too, always the wearisome one, too Herculean with the names for things. You kept a thesaurus near the fountain pen, rough handled synonyms into deplete messages, all the while you necked me, your Cerberus, thrice to reach my eyelashes. I never told you then, I tell you today, those translations were wretched, your adjectives overwrought. But what will I erase of you tomorrow? What do I keep of us, now that seeds have rotted? You said *tomorrow will always be late in arriving*, you said you ever liked being the negation of negation. From your well, love swole against me. I was not so torn, you said, as unborn, wanted to be always womb bound, to speak the imperative. I cannot stand to leave you, as I had left you before, on so many instances. I rose, wanting to leave, must as much as I could endure, if not for anything but obliged reason. I got as far as the door, the room moved through you to arrest me, your irrational animal. One last theft, glimpsing a half book of matches, a splintering bookshelf, the portrait of Jacqueline, three butts in the ashtray, the objects of forgetting, then objects of an impaired construction. I approached the stairway. Your footsteps will strand you, you said, each regrettable step, a long spiral down, like Claudel's ear, Ponge's snail shell. It followed me, the said. I brought it back, found your back was to me, sitting at your desk, so you are back to me, you said, fondling the writing instrument, sucking it like a Belicoso. My mouth turned purple, anticipating your reproaches. I was utterly useless, curious about barren understudies for "the word." I erased myself to build you whole again, you, the troglodyte inside a skyscraper, fucking the sky like the freedom tower. Fuck it, you said, keep everything, keep the seams, the stories, keep statuesque, tour the galleries of my modern atrium, for you to me, and I to you, will never again be so brazen, so raucous, with the names for things again. You said to love you is to run my tongue like a tide over your dismembered appendages, littered and lithe. What is love but your action of violence toward me, mine toward you, hips all volley and aquake? With a remote you turned on Bach on the stereo, glided your fingers across your sternum, strummed an invisible harpsichord. I was there, you waited for me, at my last verge, when I was temporarily gone on errand, collecting contraceptives and limbs. Love was always scathed. Time, you said, is death at work on eternity. You intended to love and to play in the shade, you insisted to carve, to caress with a blade, to keep the hours etched.

My feeblest dear, you said, always troubled by matters of the heart, when it is my hands, gone from their hinges, and my phallus, castrated, that you should look after, gather, torch. Phalanx of words for your beloved kept. Never mind metonyms, you said, you have no longer nerve for them. I love you, you loved me, like a reflexive verb and lacerated, haunted, shivered, in every tense, the object that every time returns. Still, even as sleep has no answer for love, you say little, little that is not wary, say little as if singed, except that tomorrow, as it happens, is our anniversary, when I came back home with sale items from the grocery store, stale loaves and pitted olives. I raise the pail you had installed with a pulley system, quite primitive but ingenious, so I could stir you about hither and tither with a ladle, whenever the occasion befell me, like the baboon in the witch's kitchen, bring you to my blemished lips. I sip you, you are something sour, you embitter me. I banquet at your desk, the desk you now absent, pressing the crumbs I had left into any three of my fingertips, fiddle them to oblivion with my thumb, to not invite vermin, to not leave behind any further evidence, of my having been. All the same my stare at your back languished you, your features and verse, you had gotten old so lifeless. You said death gave love design, that love is a sphere, there are diameters yet to journey and reply to, discount wire bins in the rain to rummage through. I am walled and rung alive by your love, your love annihilated me from the territory of circumferences, of your retina. The pen, it always smoldered, your affection was Thracian, and I to such great extents restless, in you I am wallowing. I dwindled a time so desperate, you were my precious calamity. Time, with you, was so many a moon. Time, with you, it ensues dearest. Do you remember? Remember me at my reptilest? I promised to fear death yet to die having known your hands so shatteringly put me to rest. You said you promised to endeavor for me magnificent steps toward a temple of the sun. I swore to always search the firmament of your irises. You swore words altogether insufficient, I have only to fail to utter them, so that for you I am utmost. A promise will never be enough, you said. I lost you just as I attained the threshold, turned away from, paced. I nearly touched something beautiful, but it was bygone. Love and death, a just war, the event of my trespass. The clock above your desk continues to toll armless hours, my bereavement, silence and dust film a lack of presence. I am a catalog of collected sand and sadness, all paradox and harmony. I bear life only with glances. Art was curbed with the urinals and shoes, cracked television screens, motorless blenders, the usual discard, burn wounds by baptism. Literature is not enough, but you sustained to whisper bastard couplets. *I breathe you / day and night I breathe you.* Take a breath, and break. I maw unmarked pages, reopen the chapters that you had left unfinished, to risk repair, escape, a proxy to proximity with you, wound. You see, the lacerations have cut too deep. The mouth my lips first greeted was not where it should be. You said this was what it was to know hunger, beyond was anguished. I take too much care with your apparition, you said, you will see, the forsake of me. On the clothesline were fastened skirts and stockings and ties, you wore partially dried socks that climbed to your knees and I grew out my hair, the length of it I will always remember you by. I was your adored hide, the one you later threw your other lovers down onto, a lascivious eclipse you nearly performed on me. Maybe you have. You said *you seal you fascinate them / you cover me,* the said ever stammered, stolen. From whom does your extinction of me speak? I knew what comes next. You violined my hip, it's over there, your old desk leg of calcium, petted me on the pelvis pacifically with rosin, I knew what might happen if I let you finish. I reclined into your stomach, an oceanic pit, leaning like the entombment, congealed hot sauce still scalding my chin. We spent that anniversary together, the last we partied, collaging what we had salvaged from the gutters. Our love was fated an incomplete monument, the likeness of a half-formed postulant. Of this we were in affinity, in ripples, in a tremor of effigy. I tucked myself into folds of your mica and feldspar robes, hooded and headless underneath the masonry, like Masson's Vitruvian man, claiming inspiration. I realized then, for the first time, the first of hurts, exiled on an island of ash and adhesives, that your war was not with love, nor even with I, as for me it had been so with space, with sleep, but with geometry, the regularity of shapes, abstract speech and homesickness for caves. You never flinched when I went with my tongue for your navel, steered against other discreet cavities. I mistook fear for living, and I remain so fearful, writing your initials into layers of scorn and shame, I, who was always so shamed at your touch, reared an erotic horror, nearly something beautiful. I feared no longer life, I saw what that had inspired, where that got me, but myself as I feared you. In the morning, after we breakfasted in bed on toast and hanged to dry your garters, we found Jacqueline leaning against an iron fence. *I discover you I invent you / sometimes you deliver yourself.* This is not a body to defile, with which to trifle, you said, grazing goose pimples on the masonite, as I traced Marilyn's nose with a scissor, cutting for unexpected meetings and painful echoes, incoherent and ravishing. The knife is pursuit, you said, I wanted only to hunt the crescendos of you. In so doing you enclaved me, here, butchered, in words, the monolith of your foyer. You put the canvas down, drew from your pocket a foam-rubber stress ball, the left eye of Oedipus, groped it piecemeal, and I battled a vacancy of gazes. Jacqueline was not a muse, you said, she was the cliff diver of mad love, perhaps not famous enough to prohibit her pictures, by Claude, Dora, Pablo, without legal permission, least of all her husband's, who was still distraught by the beach in Brittany. You said André knew love as anatomy but could never quite take that leap, while Antonin felt the precipice, felt he lived in a world of seductive plummets, without the safety of a railing. Those objects glimpse back, love is the felt of forever ago, and I have taken to chewing on pen caps. You lust my damage, well, I love you collaterally, an incest, I am inbred, an egg within your mania of cubes. I need you, I needed to say you, you prey me, I pray you keep reading. But you interrupt me, I am without, your dialectical undoing. I was your biological ruin, your pliant endless becoming, the times that I think of you, tanned me, your luscious cadaver. You pulled the pelt around my face, in profile across your lap. Your words were meteoric, wore the contours of comets, left craters upon my cozy futile flesh, my skin pockmarked and Picasso. I listened to you, you reinvented me, you continued, love is heresy. All the while Jacqueline stands in the corner, posing for a friend whom she had met at design school. There is the unmade flapper in her face, whose cosmetics have by the time of her photo shoot been drained and dried around the eyes and lips. A grapevine of curls, which catch the light of a sunrise at her nape, belongs to Augustus. One is too distracted to realize her chest is bare, the left breast nearly or undecidedly nippleless. Later she would wear long shawls like her friend Frida. To another friend, who planted sunflowers at the entrances of crypts, she recalled her elsewheres. An arrow sits there on the canvas, superimposed and unsteadily. It is unmistakably, unremarkably Cupid's, dipped not in gold or lead but blizzard, an ivory void replaces its rouge. The base of the fletching, neither cock nor hen feather, fits ergonomically with the outward curve of her thumb, the shaft closest to the tip rests delicate upon the edge of the index finger. Jacqueline is aestheticized from behind a pane of glass, like Ortega's garden. Her witness is almost ghostless against her back, tidal, tuft, and swan. It orphans her again, the arrow, yet there is no redress. Jacqueline, the underwater dancer, sunbathes on the roof of the coliseum, she regards the wake. *I write you / you think me.* Love, you have said all that I can take.

SOON TO BE

This way now same as last way then, the head bent filled with all those phrases been, unsure if aloud I've just said them, slipped past out into the light looking not as they were conjured in the shadows, falsely recalled, a murmur I'd intended to revive as I went, but failed to summon, either way strayed, I wander with them, the words, rustles, wrecked by distances kept near yet not quite, and I separately absent, at midday again, with the chores for the afternoon done, I won't list them, now tomorrow undone, I walk in such regard, a torn-about pace, the nights risen, then of course the sun, so many times neither to me, so it be the needless sceneries, that elapse what I've said, yet the whim keeps me moving, as I go, come toward, approach, now gone away from a glimpse, the phrases etch faint inscriptions, remembered all wrong the error echoes, but this way now the phrase patterned, the route never plotted, the words imperfectly hung, tacked disorderedly to my head, even in a place as crowded as this, unraveling precipice, an image pixelates, granularly, as I keep going on, passing by me, the blurs of windows, balustrades, pastel curtains quaking in their frames, underexposed but coming into focus, I see a shutter thrown open, the veranda I delayed my sight on during winters, waiting for when the ivy will resume to overtake it, pastel curtains hemming and hawing their borders, the outlines behind them evading shape, the phrases turning, ever so slightly, but on the image I'm lingered, a delicate instant, I've missed them entirely, the words, that is, shards, or pursued from too far off, trying to draw a bead on when, at once, sudden, *now something of the world creeps in*, I hear her say from the edge of the balcony, in Andes, raised on a slope by pillars of cypress, *there has to be something of the world that persists*, and I travel past the words as I lose sight of her, from the bottom of the hill, as I lose her there a silhouette to the sun, but I try to follow them, the words, riven, before they blend into the oblivion, when that summer, in Andes, we believed it was the nearby spring from which the sound of falling water ranged, but it was only the breeze, the remnant of rain, the long approach of cars from some distant highway, that we couldn't see from the cabin, the property, past the canopy of trees, when around the corner, on Nevins Street, I am brought back by a pigeon that has landed at an elderly man's feet, he's seated on a bench, residing on the far end, he is the far kind, his hands resting on top each knee, legs spread apart evenly, his posture not of leisure, where the space he leaves for another to take occupancy, to seize indefinite respite, is unbearable to me, he has only the pigeon to distract him, it doesn't, it's as if the pigeon has mistaken him for a stone, some cast figure, reproaching me in his stillness, the pigeon trespasses the stretch between his feet, standing still beneath him, and a little more with shame I renew the lilt of my steps, run my fingertips against a chain-link fence, tiptoe atop a network of concrete honeycombs, it seems a reticulum, with one foot after the other I stride the flaws of its design, the empty capacity between points, when the elderly man's face tilts in my direction, I do not meet his eyes, as I walk by, at pebbles the pigeon pecks, grips a piece of gravel in its beak, staring, as so often I have done, as the elderly man does, alert but blankly, as I pare rust from the fencing, my heels quicken, soon to be out of sight, in Andes we took rock paths to hidden cusps neither of us knew the location of, I couldn't hear her over the sound of our footfalls, the words in disrepair, she again elevated above me, I heard a drum beating, somewhere in the forest, on the trail, it kept my legs nomadic, I do not know where we are going, just out of the copse, Nevins begins to incline, now north of the canal bridge, when I see her on the mezzanine it means, no please, no more meaning, it absences, it empties, it brings to light that I am leaving, that I am going somewhere her goodbye will soon get to, the where of some I go, as I hear her say *see you soon*, but I know, I know the sadness caught in her throat, ringing in my head, I know something of the world creeps in, slips out, as the phrase lessens to faint of breath erelong faded, but the words, tremendously unvoiced, will soon to be rekindled, delivered threadbare, *soon you see*, lifted was the balustrade in Andes, lifted is she in memory, how she stood there against the sky, the sky pausing for her hands, her hands resting forgottenly on the railing, content to hang in the fore, to have no purpose whatsoever, wearing the wilderness around her, memory banks I keep replenished, so I might sleep ceaselessly, dreaming she is Eve in Andes, at the bottom of the hill, there is creation in her stare, a process of tides and waves that formulate from the glare, I would know by now the terrain, the stars, the ways of where I have got here, but something about the encounter, the arrival, remains unfamiliar, ensuing to be she becomes, and here I am, then I was, avoiding with seamless motion fissures in the pavement, when another phrase reaches me, the image reminisced, these marches have at least taught me patience, they teach me that I have worn out life this way, burdening city sidewalks, burning forests, performing no more else than chores, then doing them again, keeping alive the images soon to pass, from here, from there, from this, until the phrases again change, ever so slightly, climbing up the hill, the columns of cypress leaving splinters in my palms, as I brace myself to them and look above, from underneath the floorboards of the balcony, where the shadows give shape to her body, according to the light that intervenes, that defines her, narrowly, through their crevices, I go left so as to go further away from here, from home, this way less inhabited, though it's the way the sun's fated to maneuver, so be it me as well, but still I make time to dwindle, to wear grooves in the sidewalk, to roll up another smoke without ever losing a step, but caught suddenly by surprise, to see this is where the canal ends, when I had thought it extensive, *soon you see*, that last way then repeating, the balcony abandoned, Eve working late, I forget how she earned her living, but I see her, sometimes during the evenings, when she spotted me hiking up the heap in Andes, tall grass stung my calves and shins, the blades giving me rashes she would later tend, have to medicate, dress with rags drenched in balm, it still burns, so we turn in for the night, not to go outside again, not until the following morning, when the sun is risen, crawls up the sheets, spills inside, through the shades we kept open, to retain the days of *poor babe, poor dear,* she says, *since when did your skin become so sensitive?* I was surprised to see the fire pit still going, surprised this way I couldn't keep going, on Nevins, a yard heavily guarded with more fences, scores of patterns, luscious vines one does not see prevail too often in the city, to which I repay my gratitude, for my requital, my anonymity, as I cross the street three-fourths of a square, head back a way to where some of I went, kick a pebble, kick it repeatedly, it strays, I decide not to pursue it, but to instead regain my usual rhythm, and to where is familiar, until another left to be made, unless I want to chance him again, the elderly man, that is, who scorns me from his bench, which might be, if I'm not mistaken, in the proximity of the shuffleboard club, that I will happen upon, with scorn of my own, another time mistaken, not now, though, not this way, but then I didn't know I'd encounter its edifice, its derision, its approximation to him, whom I might again walk past, with head bent, and learn but then again a building never meant, or not quite intended, to be occupied by the likes of me and the elderly who, in those late stages of life, ask nothing from the world but armistice and company, but the neighborhood gathers too large a crowd for peace, its clamor brought me out of other patterns, the phrase, the image, they conflate, they cement, I cannot decide now on a destination, on home or ridicule, on being noticed, so I turn left, roulette I guess, went from the busy avenue, and go north again, toward the two-lane highway, splitting in two directions, gladly less populated, carrying my fellow flâneurs, the same kind of idlers that until now I'd carefully avoided, when I'm arrived at a gas station, realizing I'm struck with thirst from walking so far, as I have come, desiccated from the long pilgrimage, to nowhere, never anywhere, in particular nowhere certain, but of course, having burned my last cigarette paper to ash, and low on shag, on corks and stems, and so unearthed by dehydration, I confront other strangers soon to fear, like in Andes, at the gas station, on route twenty-eight, the only one for miles, where rolling paper cost ninety-nine cents but the tobacco was for pipe smoking, so Eve purchased the kind I prefer, at some other gas station, some other miles away, on a different day I spent with her, in the mountains, so she could marvel at the vistas, her footfalls like a drum I tried to syncopate with mine, but couldn't find the rhythm, in the woods, she wanted to lead the way, I let her always lead, it was easier to follow, to know only the parts of her I wanted to know, then the parts became the whole of her, the calm she displays on the balcony, as she creates visions to stalk me, the phrases became deafening, when she herself remained quiet, fenced in my silence that surrounded her, still, the sky pausing for her, her hair swaying there, the wind reaching the heights of cypress, I saw the way Eve's back arched, her one hand restraining, ever so slightly, her billowing white gown, reflected in the window behind her, where she stood, when I came back from the reservoir, as usual empty handed, with nothing to cook for us, to find when I looked up, from the bottom of the hill, there, in my last line of sight, me mirrored back, separately absent, maneuvering narrow aisles, on the tips of my toes, so as not to disturb the gentle tones of the gas station convenience store, that I have wandered into nearly out of routine, bravely toward the coolers, past two strangers concealing beer in brown paper bags, the paper soaked through, the bottoms of their cans making obvious their content, halting their conversation for me till I pass, take a bottle of seltzer off the rack, away from other glistening bottles, get on line to pay, waiting, as a stranger in front of me plays the numbers, calls them out to the clerk behind the counter, as if he knows them well, as if they've let him down before, dashed his hopes until there were none no longer, only the liturgy lasting, but the stranger has to live, I credit him for that, has to give and has to take and in this exchange be nonetheless impoverished for it, announcing the date his father died, his mother's birthday, *soon you'll see*, the anniversary of his marriage, the date he divorced, the address of his childhood home, Aries for him, Taurus for her, *their signs will bring me fortune*, and we, the calmly strangers, brought together in the convenience store of the gas station, under circumstances of torrent inebriations, share in common how empty we've become, how bored, the beads of sweat that the fluorescent lights, our reluctance to be known to each other, bring out atop our bodies, beads of sweat over our lips, across our foreheads, as I put down the bottle of seltzer, where the condensation leaves a crescent on the wood, count my money, there's no shag that I prefer, perhaps no point in buying papers now, but still, there is that which is always soon to be denied me, separates me in the world, me in the body, divided into unequal parts, two points of a scale, my soul-side weighs heaviest, in my toil, to delay the world, to let the image last, just a little longer, then there was I, this way I'm less careful now, toward the direction of home, I suppose it's home to where some of I go, I have before been on this road, soon you'll see, ahead, past the abutment, Nevins and Baltic Street will meet at the archery building, as I wonder if I'll wander through the alleys of the casket factory, where by the oxbow Eve is Artemis in Andes, where we try to locate her likeness in the night, but I couldn't discern the symmetry, the night circled around me, the fire I'd built began to die down, we descended the mountain before evening arrived, pointing out the landmarks she had memorized on our way up to the top, the quarry, the sound of falling water to the east, lost to me, when I had been lost this whole time, when we first scaled the cliff, she uses her hands as a smoke signal of farewell, she is the huntress in Andes, I can't see her, can't quite make her out, I track her in my head, *the name of the bow is life*, she says, *but its work is death*, the canal cascades, somewhere in the distance, it soothes me a trifle, as I slip out from rows of residential housing, I won't describe the miasma, the putrid smell, that rises from and tarries the inland channel, ending where we were alone, in the woods, but the chores were waiting, I hurry past people on the sidewalk, careful not to disturb the pace that seizes me toward home, where Artemis will return, when I myself returned empty handed, the day spent at the reservoir staring into wakes, an unstable image stares back, as my look fails to pierce the depth, in the sky that night we would only locate Orion, as I attempted to find, to follow, against a current of lingering light, the constellations, the indistinct sequins of her gown to the soft spots of her skin, reddened under the midday sun, *see you soon*, she says, and sets out to succeed in doing what I couldn't do for us, fetching something to eat, that is, when it is I who was left here, resumed sweating, though now less parched, at the traffic signal, taking the left off Nevins, waiting to cross the busying intersection, when the trouble is I return to her, to the image, to the balustrade, too late and at a standstill, in Andes to eat became an all-day affair, the walks undertook seldom beyond the borough, but in the periphery a conjectural effort, the result of which only keeps us hungry, only kept us starving, distracted, by the phrase, I won't discover it again, intact that way, when she finds later myself only a likeness, with bruised fruit I'd gathered around the perimeter of the property, bundled in a pouch I fashioned with the lower portion of my shirt, and Artemis, almost unrecognizable, covered in mud, but not quite completely, displaying the remains of a stag she had found while foraging around the outskirts of the premises, where we meet close to the quay, not anticipating I'd find her, dragging by the ankles a carcass, in the growing expanse of darkness, at the bottom of the hill, when she seldom ventured from the balcony, when I had often to find my way back without her footfalls to follow, only the image beckoning me, toward directions, distances frequented but not entirely familiar, *there has to be something of the world that persists*, she says, as there was the sky giving off its first trace of night, there is the rubbish, appliances left to residue my disrepair, there were the palisades, like any other, guarding just a glance of the ruins, there is the mass of strangers, whom I must, as it so happens, startle with my gait, whom I may somehow amuse, or arouse pity, by my way of going places, leaving spaces for interlaced lovers, and there is more to where some of I go, where some time I may stay, my mind and the main roads, but for now it spares, and ceases, until soon to be again, I hope for the last, her bleaching image of syntax.

DELIGHT/EQUAL DREAD

Here, over here. There was something here, before any of this, but now it is gone, erased entirely, and in its place, makes no difference, but it will stay, I suppose instead, I'm not sure for how long, looks like for good, maybe just for now, I will have to make it permanent, if I wish to continue, somehow, in any case. Go on with it, so be it. What would it have been like had I not denied who I was, had I let my hair grow long, wore loose-fitting clothes, didn't take up drink or smoke, never spoke, kept to myself and not the gossip, the coteries, the shame, slept and never hastened? There would still be the calm, on spare occasion, alone, the coldly being, not wishing it otherwise, warmth, that is, and the eyes, yes, always the eyes, the outlines they survey, give expression to, pervade, and, of course, the mind, which does not follow the same shapes the eyes frame, only other, distant contours, in a fog or haze, leading to somewhere elsewhere, perhaps sleep, or death, we'll know soon enough, that I follow in the silence, the shadows again, from a greater summit, that is the cavern of my dread and ecstasy, difficult to tell the two apart, keeping me still, or numb, or neutral, nothing, really. Now what else do I say? Sometimes I startle myself, but swiftly find torment again, because, in total sum, I loathe to be, really. Yes, denial, it could be loss, too, of hope, I suppose, despair, I don't know, these are just words, an instinct, don't quote me. Alas, something of me stays, here. I am an instant, drawn and quartered, there are the signs that I am aging poorly, the rashes on my feet, reaching upward on my body, the growth of excess skin in its crevices, the perspiration in my palms, the armpits, behind the bend of my knees, perpetually. But then the *before*, making its way back, it always does, no? returns a mauled form, an auspice, under the rain or in a crowded space, not as I remembered, a devastation in the face, yes, always a face returning, featureless, not belonging in the throngs or torrent, but the throes, that much is certain, or familiar, to an extent, the vision, that is, if that is what it can be called, obscurant, once an instant in itself, which I have forgotten the feeling of, keenly felt, but no longer the lack, except there were no eruptions of rashes then, I don't recall the slightest flare-up, not on the surface, at least, I was thinner, imbued with a reddish hue, better dressed and stylish, for the time, always a servant to time, and then to fashion, wearing scarves and buying potential lovers drinks I could not afford, but leaving it at that, only a gesture, really, nothing more intended, though I knew the gesture well, practiced it often on myself, in the mirror, but never exceeded it, that is, emptiness, I prayed for different outcomes, never having the courage to ask if I might walk them home, stay the night, I suppose, with my drunk crushes. Some things have not changed, at least, there is still the persistent terror, always being afraid, now of different things, which probably don't exist, not in time, anyway. Those were instants now erstwhile, I know a few others, but I am unsure if they'd really happened, the way the vision projects them. Had I only been witness? Sure enough there were other beds, audacities even, disgraced mornings I fled, but wanted to stay, it's too late, I'd been mortified, either way recreated, as the voyeur or the object, the resolute chagrin. In another time and another place, maybe. The places, yes, I can revisit them, though they are no longer intact. I arrive there again, from the well where my frenzies stir, mostly by accident, by way of different routes, longer journeys, from other entrances once closed off or unknown to me, my recrudescence more peculiar than the ruin, how it looks to me now, or is it the sensation that is odd, the sorrow, that is, of once being again at a destination that has lost its meaning on my way to it, the meaning now a memory for which there is no respite, these places that can only be described by absence. Now then, the time, I tell it by thresholds, how long to stay the image, surfaced from the instant already withered, having been the encounter, stumbled upon again, with the iron gate, rusted, opening onto the field, the park bench, immediately on the left, a memorial to a name I've repeated often, every time I sat there, waiting for no one, and the shade, all fiendishly the same as they were, as they once appeared, back then, scarcely changed, maybe the leaves have fallen the color of fall, or the sidewalk repaved, but otherwise the ache, yes, freshly dressed, of the before that is no longer, the face that fades under my faculties, the face that my eyes betray, the eyes looking at someone else, into someone else, or past someone else, really, till the mind wanders elsewhere, too, that is, goes away from here, or begins to wonder, how much time has passed? The shade stretches farther now, blending with the crepuscule without interruption, at least from me, anyway, how could I stop it? I mustn't, if I could, see clearly the way things used to be, they never were, and now the night descends on me, the way a thing always is, suddenly, or ought to be, dire, desperate, too dark to see, with the eyes and the mind, yes, both unwilling, but they oblige me, so that I can continue, in one way or another. I tend to an itch, before I can go on, walking, at least there is that, in addition to cowardice, always walking, my favored mode of travel, to the next place, farther away from, farthest out. The psoriasis has spread to the outside of my right leg, a few inches below the kneecap. If it had been on the inside of my left leg, I could, still standing, use my right foot, more accurately the innermost toe, to lessen the irritation, I imagine like a flamingo would. Instead, I bend down, in a bowed position, and relieve myself with the right hand, making marks incessantly, flakes of skin falling below the cuff of my trousers, like dust, onto my shoe and the concrete. I walk straight, still itchy but less so now, sometimes straight becomes a circle, scarcely do I walk where I have not been, but, again, accidents *do* happen, yet I am ready for them, then they aren't really accidents, then, no? I suppose not, I suppose it's not anything, maybe misfortune, or chance, or fate, probably peril, I don't believe it, though, I am discouraged, there is still so far to go, from north to south, the south is where I've dwelled, since being far away from here, after the donation of my wardrobe, on which I've spent too much, on pleasing and my guise, but walking is free, at least, I still have some savings, even after the drinks, a small sum for which I have no use, perishing. One can't stay straight forever, there are too many walls, dead ends, et al. and so on. Under these circumstances one can choose to turn or turn back, to recover the direction of a line, but I get ahead of myself. I continue straight, sweating now profusely. In my sights are horizons, the patterns of buildings, strangers walk past me, I've already forgotten their expressions, whether they paid me attention, what they were wearing, if it was flattering. I turn my eyes from them, the scene, that is, to there, somewhere over there, or in here? I don't know, another place missing something, barren, that I'd tried, intensely, to elude. I walked wide-awake here once, there was no one on the streets, they were empty, soon to be daylight, I was not alone, though, there was a group of us, but that's it, no one said a word, we let the words race inside our heads, I can't speak for them, but I am almost sure of it, there were Sequoia firs and spruces on the sidewalk, our heels fell on pines, in the rain, there were Christmas lights, yes, the only ones on in the city. Sometimes the places come to me, stay just briefly, when I am moving, nowhere, steadily straight and back the same way I'd tread, those dead ends already toured. That was before, the formerly, resembled an instant, with the eyes, if only momentarily recognized, that I can't properly distinguish, with the mind. What next? Such a damning question. There is nothing else but to turn around now, I suppose, there is still time, time enough to get lost, to try down a different road on which I can cast my doubts, and not find meaning later, yes, why deny myself, now, when I have so little? Let it be strange, poorly lit and uninhabited, with fewer people, I'll ignore it anyway, the street, that is, and of course the people, most roads rarely traveled look the same in the dark, no? I choose to count my steps instead, lose count, really, keep pace, fascinate more on the ground rushing past me, until I look up and see a pub, so that's where this was, all this time, unless it has moved from somewhere else, or there was an expansion, a franchise granted, but no matter, never been, only heard of, in neon above me, *B   S T R O*, from the window I make out a man inside, in a trench coat, wearing scarves, and someone, leaning their elbows on the bar, their face moving into glares, blurs on the window, no, I knew how to get here, but I have approached from the other side, another angle, and I know how to leave, through the side entrance, early in the evening, when someone, anyone, plied with wine, gets up to powder their nose, there is something itching me, my nerves, maybe, an urge always absent, I walk away, let the neon sign fade out of sight, keep straight.

I'M ALIVE I TELL MYSELF

Winter arrives. The cinder has come to rest over me, too, in the silent mist of it. I'm alive, I tell myself, for a little while longer at least, during these unbound and bygone days. I still struggle the anguish in my voice, the cold I wrest it from. Rest, just rest here, in this cold furrow the weather has dug, go on with it, and suffer the hours death won't complete. It is no use. Outside, around me, in every distance is something heard but too faint to interpret. Sometimes I wonder if I even hear anything at all. I lie motionless to listen with a purpose I never tire to deny myself. I am tired, though, I give it up easily, fidgeting amongst the foliage, the moss, the seethed sod. It's the same hope I hear, words spoken to me without sound but a sensation I shiver. They are my words, of course, coming from me. Soon I will also struggle for warmth, under the shade I've chosen to reside, for the time being that becomes, not unusually, longer than I intended. I'm still here, after all that has passed, and now I can see my breath in the grayscaled evening, leaving me by a listless kind of labor. When I raise my head to receive the Emu of the sky, I find instead heavenly bodies I can no longer name, disappearing behind a tunnel of trees and appearing again when the leaves have ceased shaking. With great care, repeatedly, I trace the constellations that are yet discerning, gnostic to me, and follow them before they flee, before the morning recovers them. It is no use, even if the aurora will never ascend again. My sight trains itself on the space between paling embers, gathered in the darkness, and I can feel the earth spinning on its axis. I had been sleeping, it seems, with dreams of my decease, promised to me, swarming the embers' dying glow, wanting not to restore their radiance but collapse with them on the horizon. I had come to stop here after a walk, yes, a long, lonely perambulation, or peregrination, that at first brought me elsewhere, possibly, before leading me here. For how long have I settled? Under what conditions has my roaming stayed me? It is no use. I have not the ambition or strength to get up, go on, from here to where, for now at least, but I find my ways, have always. I thought I had seen Gullfoss, the Iguaza Falls, other cliffs my eyes felled on from out of reach, but that was another time, eating away at another's marrow. I would have plummeted, but I chose the dirt over the sea, wherever my wanderings have taken me, the least hospitable, and a final resting place. I am afraid I may have missed my chance to go quietly, that's why I stay here, and wait. Despite my confusion I still have reasons, must still make excuses. I do not worry, someone will find me here, eventually, some day, maybe not. I think now I am close to ending, the streetlights have turned out, dormant, inert, cockroaches emerge to herd on my skin, it begins to snow, or is it ash that comes down, no matter, it is no use, no impetus to move. Except now my surroundings begin to frost over, and to maintain the mire for which I have grown accustom, I turn from my back onto my stomach. Numb at present, I press my face to the soil and till it with my cheek, creating a depression to fit comfortably the profile of my head. I hear a strong gust of wind with one ear lifted to the sky. Is it still night? Perhaps it is another night now, to fall once more and recur again. The grass has died here, in the slough, perhaps it was I who killed it with my body. Perhaps this small patch of lawn will grow back when the season's warmed over, or it will be given seed and sown when I have left it, in one way or another, below or a part of. For now it's hard to determine, too far for conjecture, I'd rather not say, pay any more mind to the point. Holding in my hand a small portion of surface I hollowed out from the marl, I presume the earth no longer belongs to me, crumbling to dust through my fingers. What thought will lend itself, heed me next? There's hardened mud below my eye, like a teardrop, like a teardrop, like a teardrop, I repeat, before memory mellows me, but it is no use, it's really just filth, I can be carrion now, though, unencumbered, when in my youth, under my father's roof, to keep clean was a chore to be conducted with the utmost care, or witness a harsher punishment than public humiliation. *A foul stench is offensive*, he would say, *better to be kempt in this world, don't let them see you this way.* My father, he was a wretched man whose morals nobody could comply with, I may have left because of him, but that is not likely, no, I was ill-fated to leave, without a reason but surely with blame, probably, or I was ditched, left alone, so I went. He didn't die alone, though, like I am sure to do, dirty, feculent, scorched by the cold, soon, surely, with no food or water to nourish me. Somewheres along the way I hid what little possessions I had on me, brought from the beginning or otherwise purchased along the way, begged for, thieved, found, or collected, until all that was left was the pursuit of images, real or perceived, it makes no difference. They are all but gone now, the objects and the effigies. With difficulty I can conjure them, which keeps me living, form unfaithful relics in their stead. I am unwilling, mostly, in this effort, I wish them not to be mine. I tried to leave them behind, but out of fear, or regret, someday, even remorse, I kept record of their locations, maintaining with careful detail instructions on how to retrieve them again, had my mind changed about their meaning to me. I used to believe I would want them back, to taste again the whisky from Islay, the dokha smoke in my lungs, to feel the weight of my notebook, the rough material of my laundry, to hold in my palm the silver ring passed down to me, gifted, then regained, but meaning is a brittle thing. Nonetheless the record has been lost, forgotten at the last gutter I came to rest, and for this I feel great relief rush over me. It's all memory, is it not, taking into consideration the extent to which it has been modified, over time becoming or long passed, reemerging. I would rather that which is not, when to be is to become a ditch. I don't know where I am anymore, where I will go, if I am able, if anywhere, it's no use, stay, I've made a nice little nest for myself, in spite of the temperature and the clouds, which are fine to me anyhow. Even the snow, which now coats, a thin layer, the lower region of my body. More sounds a far ways off, lulling me, guests arriving, perchance, it could happen. Feasibly it's the birds, undecided if they should flock and fly south, or the pale rider, ringing the dinner bell with his horse's hooves, more audible over the ice and rime, but no less forgiving. I can never know, anyhow, never really have known, have I. It is a short field to march. A sound draws me nearer to the soil, voices maybe, and now I am frostbitten. I have not managed my appearance so well. To weep, to weep, to weep and to grieve, would save me from perishing, but this indecency has become strange to me. It's no use, just the slightest excuse, for having lived licentious and ugly. Dying in the silence has its uses, too, when death is not a consequence but a commencement, unsaid.

THE ANIMAL OF EXISTENCE

They ask about my life. The likelihood of my living on. With eyes that will not be met I say of their inquiry that it is no decision of my own. For the most part I struggle unknown. But the world, I am privy to it yet. My silence laments into night. They ask about my life, but for life I grieve deeply. Ordinarily I'm wasting away. Staring long enough to disappear where my eyes fall their gaze. I think, in particular, of what to read next. How effortlessly, with little known danger, I forfeit these moments. On a mantle opposite from where I lie I fix my sight upon a volume, the contents of which have become bewildering. I cannot move to greet its thread, devour blindly the words it holds, but only obtain, from this grave distance, the frayed linen of its spine. I have been bedridden for some time, for some time too long. When past noon arrives the shadows shrink enough for me to remember its title, if only loosely, but it is lost to me now that rain claims the sky. They do not offer to retrieve it for me, to read aloud select passages. Instead they repeat that I will not be cured. The diagnosis drifts, means not to me regardless. My sole interest is the shapes in proximity fading in the absence of light. I would feel panic if I sought to gain recovery from my illness, fated, fashioned in slightness of breath. I recall a line, from somewhere else entirely, once skimmed over and over again, not having then intended to commit it to memory. In a language difficult for me now to comprehend, a voice familiarly foreign, *I preferred the sharpest corner of this room to be alone in.* I say this aloud and am no stranger to the echoes. I bury inside, become gestures exhuming visible patterns of smoke. Words, all those menacing words. It was by them I lived for no future. They ask about my life but I have my sight on tattered cloth, the stitching coming undone, the binding beneath. The hours pass this way, tracing outlines out of reach. I ask them will the shadows rise again, or will the days remain from me forever hidden? I knew a man once in a story. I regret not being able to recall the context that informed our conversation. But he spoke to me about decades, how to anatomize the emptiness, the spaces safe within a pause. I appeal to him now, as if beside me. Why chimneys and pillars? I ask. Before we met between the folds of lace I believed heaven an interval of stars, but it is in another's pages that I stir. Man I once knew in a story, pull the blanket up to my neck, please. It grows cold in here, I am freezing. I forfeit the lexicon, for now at least. Turn my head in a different direction, down. Nothing moves. The blanket is made of fleece and it is crimson. I am able to sleep, often choosing to do so, but rather now feel with my left hand the material beneath the covers the way I would a water's surface. Slowly studying, with precision, the imperfections with the tips of my fingers, pulling lint and balling it behind my nails until five balls are firmly in place. This is the sole sensation with which I am familiar. I met another voice once who liked to count the pebbles in his pockets and crawl about on his stomach. My legs have given way as his. That would be the story, no? The arc of which he forbade me to follow. Nevertheless I cherished his kinship. I would say to him now that it was in our distance that we were kept bound, the voice hemmed me to him, and he would reply as he always has, in a faint murmur, *forget me, know me not, yes, that would be the wisest, none better able than he.* I was always grateful for that voice. Here I am however finally destitute, collecting lint into larger pellets that I, once they harden, let fall to the floor not felt physically for some ages. An unexpected warmth prompts me to resign this habit. I pull my arms out from under the quilt. Unkempt and unprotected they have grown ashen, hairless. I lick them for the taste of salt though my glands have long ceased to salivate. Something like the sun emerges again and I return, instinctively, to the volume on the mantle. But at dawn it is yet too early to make out the letters. What dawn is it that descends on me? If I try hard enough I could make out the rubric that the words, one after the other, form to complete a phrase, but I wish not to exert any effort in this regard. All I've managed is a few hours passed, the news having long since reached me. I wait, wasting away, for some reunion, when so much of myself goes abandoned, bruised. The more I repeat myself, the more my origin accumulates. One of the words comes back to me in vague recollection: Melancholy. If I had the will I would see it writ, but as such I can only feel it, sense it somewhere memorized. When I attend to sound I listen to the spring of a fountain. From the mouths of marble goddesses are whispered the secrets of stillness. I say "melancholy" loud enough to fill the room with a sound that just as soon becomes strange to me, and remember I had a name. They say it on occasion. I call out again, "melancholy!" "melancholy!" so I will not forget as soon. They ask about my life, I ask them what name was given. They say *not until we have heard a logical response.* I say again "melancholy," which has been reclaimed on the volume across from me by an acute shadow, but the reason for my utterance is lost. I begin to describe to them a different fountain, bathed in fragments of light, its basin drained. Beneath the copper patina fade the figures of Wisdom and Felicity. I specify the stone in fall. Along the way they stop listening, or maybe I've stopped speaking, reminded of an image. A woman in silk, throwing torn pieces of paper over a balustrade, watching them float like falling snow, unburdened by a breeze, down to the street below. Another line repeated: *one word is not enough to save the rest.* There is winter in my eyes, and a tempest in her breast. We have never met, not in flesh, but I revisit her at random standing on the balcony that way. Sometimes I am next to her, fixing my posture, apart from. She is gone now, and I beside her. Birth. Birthing. Birthed. Another part is forming now. Have I finally adjusted my vision to the darkness? Perhaps I get the title confused. My appearance is phantom, I read it in braille, administer feature to my ailments. Seldom do I move. A far cry from this body. I struggle to shake my feet free from beneath the blanket. They come loose, triumphantly gnarled, a grotesque violet. Toes exposed cold. I am otherwise healthy, despite the coughing fits that sometimes seize me. Remaining in one position makes less severe my respiration. Have I mistaken Melancholy for Impossibility? Night falls. I remember all those tomorrows promised but never certain to me. Tomorrows will end over my eyelids. The night, at least, settles over me peacefully. They say my name and it is a siren. Include now "deaf" in my diagnosis. I am aware of one window in my quarters, from where at times a draft comes in. I know of it when it is morning, that there is a curtain quaking in its frame. I am not well enough to be near it, although I have never had urge to look outside, to know contest or pleasure, errands or engagements. All desires wane. I awake on a different day. The volume appears furthest yet away from me. I am restored to periphery, in the world, no? I am life enough, I think. It is likely enough. The borders, the balustrades. My mind speaks for me, on my behalf, I recognize the accent, it's company enough. More company than they, disappeared behind the drapes, come back only to amass what life I still manage, had hoarded before the sickness struck. The drinking den of my head. Palms upon a cold steel railing, with hydrangeas hanging over a fire escape. Their leaves lean into me in the wind, touching me lightly. I caress the fabric to mimic the texture that for a minute seems exciting, and mock the imagined. The voice, in the story, doesn't imagine. I wait for him when we are far again. I linger eternities. They refuse me still, fetch not the volume I am unable to procure alone. I fault them for their selfishness, a fault of my own. I've been known to mince and mingle words that theretofore have had no business with each other. Still instant, departed, is the condition of the volume, constant to me. The book too is faithful presence, just barely holding on, have nothing. They say my name and it is reverb, when the reflections continue, less readily. My name decays, and dies down. What to read now. The ceiling, maybe. I picture it in the dark ivory toned and damp, with its leaks like veins, cratered, a tactile map. Suddenly I am tired, so exhaustedly so, tired of the evening, the eves of dawn again. The issue unresolved, I have one, it is none. The last word, Toil it must be, with all my weariness a mirage. Where the rip of the spine ruptures the insignia, the structure, like a body behind a flame, a wave of heat. Never been, never restless, not so moved. The story emptied and never-ending and none of significance. I've wanted to say something for a while, for a time, but it would mean nothing to me now, to anyone, the mantle, the coffin, to make haste with speech or impassioned remark or ardent motion or choke or grief of any kind. They go by several names themselves, but all escape me, something else of mine ceases. The sinews show. I too am held together by shreds.

but not without the

potential of death

for it's the night of you who have died inside you awakening

—Kim Hyesoon

RUSTBELT

Here is why. Why is not. Nor yet. Why not here inhabit? Where here why I am not until. Not so much. Peel the rust. Much not so. Call that unabiding. After a while. Here where is night must be, and nor I with it resided permanently. Just. Only thus a mournful visage. An accessory. To sightlessness. Shimmering thus. The where of must without light. In the nowhere. Must be the none. Somewhere in the wherewithal have lived I. The not thus becomes. And the wherewithal needed still of life. Still of night. Yet sustained. Call that living. At any rate gasps kept going. Laboring as such endless annihilations. Life hereafter. In it nor yet woke deceived. Unabided. A beach, littered with bodies. Night combed its dune for limbs. Nearly grazing the shape of I. Moreover feasible. In the where here still remaining. Disobeying gesture. Call that genesis. Disaster hereafter. As I disobeing voice? I just barely. Formlessly the wherewithal pierced. Work sorrowfully the enterprise. Night tempered death. But death nonetheless. Howbeit. Night not I called many things. Scales played on the stars, for instance. Night accenting. Hammering keys. Yet I reach in the dark, fumbling the vastness. For I to take hold. Call that loving. Life sought in Cimmerian shadows. Describe I like a simile here. Neither I not yet. Still and all. Devastatingly so. Where here night is sterling. Nor I its siege. Here where echoes tremble thus. Must night be so voluminous, and yet I corroding russet so? Into grains. Not I yet's homeless gaze. Barely I just barren. Just an idea of I. An ideity of I? Yield to thus. For it is nothing and significantly it must become. Call that I's best effort. Then. Endlessly. What happens then here? The desert of I the night. A mirage. An adornment. Staving the light. Staying the darkness. Grazing the starry expanse. The immensity yet not I. Nearly only. Nearly, nearly. Almost all but. Where does it end, and commence thus then? When end then not yet. Then when yet not ends. Yet then end when I thus commence. End remaining this way until who. When who then inhabits here permanently. Where here night abides you. Scale I not thus. Then you must. Exercise your limbs across I of mustn't be. None I then. Here is where resided I. I never. Never I is what you call it. I what is not. What I not is. Name I less then. How until I barely somebody. You reach the sum of how barren I've become. Disembodied. A shore. I until then being eroded a length just yet you held there. Wearing away the granules. I of which there becomes no proof. Etch I in the tide. The night a precipice, and the yet of I its breadth. I limbs never formed. Thus you must settle for less. Who less settled. I then slavish there. Where there the for instance of here then until. How you beat on I the range of night. Strike I night's metal strings. The fundamental parts. Echoes on the sandbar. Press upon the mass vastness. The I yet neither. The I you beseech explain Iself. Must you why the I incomplete? The incipient must remained. Endlessly wearing at the wherewithal. Tiring then against until. The deficient must maintained. Mantle I in a serenade. The immeasurable sings sorrowfully of its vacuity. Call that coaxing life into next. So you nix I better yet to temper. I the neutralizing force to the where with all. I the void that would not be given resiliency by adding substance nor flame to it. Call that cavity. Rot. I of not. I is not. When reach not further yet nor desperately, but deepest. I thus just innermost. I again then not. Thus only a mournful ornament. Lunar. Denuded. There is more of I to lay barely. Being such your enterprise. The business of I's inhabitance, amidst annihilation. I the night impoverished. The light reaching I already extinguished. I its refuge. The wherewithal half lit. You dare a name for I to give a meaning of it. The I not become neither is. What not is I. I the wherewithout. Call that why. The night I rust. Scales just charred stars in the distance. Call I what you must. I you will call then me. A measure. Me shored thusly. Like a note played on the rustbelt. Ensue I so. At intervals of echoes a reflection rendered. Within every pause. A moment's rest upon me in disgust. I in torturous succession. Being loss evolve into me. Call that a plea. Dear how dare you. Starve I here this way. Yet how you hunger to give me shape. The ocean its landscape. Between I. No? Between me. Yes? Exclamation and determiner on the merge. Unified by a mark meant for puncture. Whereas the question I am, the tenor not. Like here and where. Unrendered. Rusting appendage of absence. Safely here nevertheless noiseless waves. You call I safe. Enough to be spoken of aloud. Into the receding sand that has you still and away from. Nor shore ever reached. How fear you I to end. But I never the less. Drag the sea. Misapprehend then. Said? Just organ sounds. Murder me name spoken. Silence speech enough. Yet for us. Here. Receiving. No/yes reaching. In the night in I for light least impaired. Say me a pale dim glow that died to get to you. Why is more of I to bear. Whereabout within. Then some ways yet can't I be tantalized. Continue I in this condition of life thereafter latent. Say I the least pure. Call that humanized. Not called so plenty. Known none. Some nowhere such as then. Same nowhere just as now. Why none here. Here why is. I the why here nearly. You the how where dearly. Why and how we welded. Night is how I must keep it. In place into pieces. The seam of the interval. The stifled echo. Festering star. When and then sewn into night. I become an ambiguity. Say I a wound instead.

TREADMILL

Then so there you are on which I can throw nothing more. So we then meagerly contour the lessening of I feeling into you contrast. Me there then so brief through you so we transparency. Stare hollow and plead merely what is left then into pieces. I leave you to happen there strewn to pace among me bated. For sounds startle you there of our silence song. But I already then more gone. No more of you what of me less than so utterly vanquished. Of us ago a moment faintly. Allow then there only your tread and grow from me intervals. Back forth then back again for what breath brought out of us vanished. Locate a rhythm in the being forgotten. Gave I to you then a gaze seeing only the solely of we. Give you to feel the thing as already traces among them I given us to falter. We be possible may be. Hush then no longer so exhaled the quietus of the mill. Traipse to write you into everything. Halt there. Wind your eyes into vacant gapes. Now stand there in the stillness of so long ago unrelieved. There excise me then erase it. I lead it quickly back to that. To pauses. Sway and raise the glass in your hand urgently to my lips upon my return trip. Raid me of your glimpses mere shadows. Spilling I from objects into avalanches on the wall. Move now on forth to back once again invisible thresholds like I never departed. What you remains left. But you menace me then into every step. Such things so I deem we to repeat desperate. And you already used to it. I robe you in rags for the ritual and the dance of cloth your pace creates for we to stride litany like. Now try to save some of I in each tug on your tatters. Each heel that you collapse in displaced accents. Then pirouette to confront the vague mirror of the window I looking gossamer. In this gesture lost to you I detect some grace. Draw a razor to my attention of it. Decrepit me if it's the last thing we ever fulfill. But plead one line at a time. I fending for us there a punctuation. The drink you gently spin from a tendency in our happening. Feel me an orbit now lade into you at every sip. There I seep you swung. My routine to march you and in so doing wear into the last thing of us were. Present imperfect tenses. When I sense me a crisis rising in your throat. A nervous tick to and fro. Looking off into somewhere that isn't you and I dragging yourself along. Now about-face there us unabled. Leer the pattern to have spun another. Thought of I as you fled the spiral. I thought of you am I formerly. Here there then gone what left to do. Trade one last measure done us in sequence. *What is it?* It is I filling pages. *With what?* My weaknesses. *When will it end?* When the sheet is bare. *Then why begin?* Because nothing is without frailty. Ah. You are there once recently stood now sited off into elsewhere. It happening in our propensities. I turn there your attention inside where all is shadow saw and pour. Then there you darken I. The drink in our hand somewhere else abruptly sup. Face about floor vanquished abroad. Now gaze vacantly at your feet that led me there. Gaps fill we. Never mind. So I ambulate into you then. I your faltered sighting. It is impossible to count my steps in your chest. Seep within you every cavity. Inhale me hollow. And you already used to it. Leave you there surrounding me like this ensconced. To borrow parlance. So there remember I am writing then playing cursively with your perforator veins. The colander body I sieve into strained. My corruption of you disarms us feeling through I like the ice melts in your drink. Choke back me down relieving your posture gestated. Inside you helical our head swarmed. You upright there fussing to make sense of me then. Clench myself with your fauces when at first I washed over you like rain on your shield. But I your thought not fled unsure the much longer we can take. You who once pondered better of me as none at all. I am better there I am you swear it. The long ago so unrelieved. You won't get the better of we who once thrived so long on monotony. Ah. When everything of you hurts I am to blame. That you say time is not an invention but felt in the sinews. The rust and the dust and the ache and the lethe. I speak to we again what is left. Where do I look? *There, in the direction of the window.* What is it that I should find? *It is you must tell me.* I see the yard let go so unruly, the mountain behind the deluge, a fog lifting from the meadow into storm clouds that have gathered above, and the faintest signs of life stirring in the wake of mist. *Now train your vision on the inadequacies. Report.* But what is my motivation behind this monologue of mad inquiry? *REPORT.* I see raindrops collected on the screen like a honeycomb; a confused mass of pearling water, vapor, light and pall. I see it belatedly. I fell transparent there into you then at our feet more restlessly. Feel me at the veil of pane this well I built inside you. The body bivouac on which I tinge. Because yours gives mine shelter. And shade. Since yours is mine to wade through. The heart attack I feel approaching belongs to you. Ah. So much to fill you with. I already tense you participle on the page. The fog faraway azure behind the bars. The last thing I brought back from memory. Trespass you to write I done. Your visit to my asylum. So sorry I your sorest corpse necessity. Tread to pen you into everywhere.

You bring it back to that. Any amount of staring to condition the incandescence from which there I came. Ah. Has to be that. Into the riot of your disappearance I apparent. Exerting the effort of great distance not going anywhere. Standing still you feel the labor of I on end. You feel it too in every tread. When each pace leads away in exchange for its return. But how much longer can we take. Your body I am buried alive. Yet you renew I outside in your sight line. Walked toward and never reached. Ah. But in so teasing reachable. In view away from. Because you beg I to end it. Bare it will never be. Handle me as if without. Curtains for us both. Because to you the body then keeps humanize survived. Because I have died for less by the conveyor belt. Compatible only since we suffer us both. In which you wear myself out a permanent blemish on the sill. No. We need not speak again. I say through you interpreting my silence. Starved you too late. Famished will do. Image me a torrent. The rags hanging on you loosely. The downpour rolling off me every effigy. We allow you the last word. *Is it you I bear down?* Hear me out. Then the body there past due.

YEARS

Lullaby chimes for a kiss trapped in my lungs. Send respiration into atrocity language. You must pry for pauses. The suspicious instances of gone most arrivals. I have that itch again and I smoke near the hearth wearing my striped sweater, sucking also at a cough drop. My mind is frayed firing menthol into my eyes to combat the combustion I feel against words. Each of my words dwindles its inheritance. In whose state am I your summer monolith? Singed chrysalis sighing the rune of blind monarchs into swine etiquette. The pious posture of wallow and wilt inaugurates my sprawling of narrative debt. The dehumanized is all too human and I am a part of you ineligible to be loved. My entrances are a revolving door. The muse enters without the mantle of her matriarchal Melos. The momentum teases the simultaneous exit. My sick lips are inoculated and shocked into an audition for you. Mine is the form that crisis takes. The hearth is warm with harm and outfitted with the nearest shape of a sorrow. Imagine a throw rug decorated with the teardrops of kindling. Imagine androgynous exhaust performing ballets up the chimney. Imagine the concierge counting the revolutions of your undying denouement. What is the plot of the inferno ceremony. Who is there to worship now that you've been bled out by Pig Cupid's arrow. Imagine an encounter that goes unreported by language.

WANDERLUST

Dromomanic thoughts the rhythmic pounding. I head due norths others have sought seeking fresher blister sounds. I've found them all but wanted to believe I had not. I no longer know what to believe except that I'm spent from limping and return. How lucky I was wishing luck now, believing only in the blast, the invocation solely to echoes. The wish to where knowledge has taken me from, back to the place we begun, the panting. My mind appears to mercy. You ought to know I'm no novice of the compass or the cardinal. Nor the sad bed of the oriole's song. There are numerous tunes but just one you keep repeating not to lose. I hear that buzzing too. These baffled buzzing magnetized eves. They've followed us as we've followed it, for a source. Thinking with baffled eyes it's a refrigerator. An air conditioner. The internal abyss of a cave. Ah, the deepest depths are the most perilous and nourishing. Before you lose it always trying to find them. But you need snug shelter and the incessant habit of blind sustenance. The cave is a dangerous place after all. For us and all other animals of prey. Even the marred dark has prayers for hiddenness. And there I am myself found as soon forgetting, already forgotten. Hunt lyrics around my unfolding headdress. Images within, objects without. Appearing to me only merciless tracks. Who else but mine partial imprints pointing in opposing directions. Trout spine. Mannequin arm. Buzz saw. Pigsty. Quaking aspen bending toward the thunderhead afar. This old dog that I am. Remembering the white bark a long ways off. Still leaning from the squallish strain crossing into long-ago yards. Lusting after so many long agos we've walked the familiar song of corn sores. Tuning these thoughts to the endangered mating call. Painting the cave. Trickling into ice trays. Manic friends of mine I wanted to believe would last. But what do I know, wishing like this, against the so many lusts of others come before. Ah, the score does not end here. It could but won't. I've located this moment the conductor's wand in the underbrush. Recoiling nearest his last footprints. Assuming the arrangement of tunneling wings. Heels that had clicked twice and waited for a miracle to occur. Awaiting. Dallying. Delaying. The miracle hadn't and the madness slips. On second thought instead recurs. Point of which no thought. At least not one found that remains. Otherwise I should be torn limb from limb. It ought to be. Seeking rhythm pounding blisters in the amnesia. What becomes of this becomes its nil. North meets its inverse and I again my mania afresh. To delirium you appeared. Your tentacles touch all at once. Advancing aberrant orientations you acknowledge the angle's blade. The future is not forlorn for us. A reason ventures thought lesser. I think the habitats frequent and conceal my steps with leaves that will be tossed by the wind. Inevitably. Headed nowhere. The body reclining in the moderate air. Listening to the perishables keeping cool. Going to sleep with the encompassed hum. No, it's not an appendage. Joins us to no one. The images are within, the objects without. Seen seeing inwardly. With welts we wander endless the sounds of my hollow den. The insulation of the cold storage is not a secret kept by anyone. I know, repeating the freeze forever.

IN MEDIAS RES

No more to this than hoarfrost. Catacomb incantation. Every word is terminal winter in my citadel embalming enjambment. While the husk over me burns I'll be forever influenza. The fever of solstices. Melting coldly surfeit with my little Moscas around me. *Mother, the mayhem, show me mercy, I can stand it I can't stand it, you're so merciless, teach me the solitude of a stone in waters no more hardened but on their way, on their way.* To the dead man's dismay. The stone that will be again by then smoothed. When ends premeditated and fated another sedate rotation. Depth hatched its unforgiving climate. Talk me out of it or let me drown. It's that soothing temporal sound. The way the world spins unlistened to. Despair is not knowledge of death, but the acknowledgment that tempts me to attempt life. *Choose.* Between sky and earth. Heaven and hell. To which I am closer. Which am I closer to. I eavesdrop on the corpse cacophony. Its moldered deliverance. Boredom baited. Breached belief. Blasphemous boulder. I adorn the dead one's crown atop the severed heads of noons. *Mother, how long will I last like this, metamorphic? Which is it I should fear more, the rain or sun? Which will preserve me less, like this, as I renovate the chambers of my palace, polar and sweltering? Can the afterlife before these hours in doubt be whom is yet as cold as I?* Questions on every corpse's mind. Surging still and tethered. To tempering currents. Perspiration fertilizing prosimetrum god's acres. Now within, now within. But too inflamed to climb out from the damp interior into malice winds. I heretic crave the rapids. Crave turbulent temples. Thistles garden the gapped space of ribcage. Unattainable florets. Arid streams. Insects stampede cosmogenic sockets. Life gains around me, without me. Years join the dead one. Vines join to vines. Ice is born of ice. I no longer tell myself I'm alive at the top of a deprived throne. Precipitation seeding prosodic mind that is time itself. *Father, was there ever a choice? Tell me, what is the most comfortable position, to lay my cheek on the surface of moons, present of all eternity?* The herring stormed within for protection. They will be my stone's pulse when time and temperature moil by chance their imbalanced chemistry. Pebbles beard my germination. To the fossilizing face I speak the speech of death. In process. Pity of proximity. *Lover, tell me no more words, in them nothing to be found, except what they've lost, impossible words name impossible worlds, I'm given back to the earth emptied, grounded I greet groundlessness.* Absent of life but not without the potential of death. Murmur of the stone grinds on atop river's winter drought. Inside schools of fish dance their own survival. Last catalyst. Impervious to the void. I am. The imperative of the dead one. You are. Antifactual embedding artifact. Pain remains the possibility. Only, entirely. The ongrowing end is what exalts me. Continuous transience. Continuous disappearance. The out of that is within. The interior beyond him. But I yet kept. Fungal cockroached and carrion. Sobbing icicles. Watering the decomposition. The hesitated poem. Finitude attitude. Hardened again, hardened again. The sound no longer draws me nearer but flocking into animal architectures. Desiring dismemberment. *All, tell me, when will it end? When it will end, I intend to go on, like this, descent into coldness cognizance.* Life dies in debt to linearity. Death lives my life for me approaching poetry.

Negation belongs to nature same as I as the dead one attended. Shovels and spades find me indissoluble and nothing. Into this moment I am insofar petrified. The cleanse foul and dirty. But too I learn to find inside deplete radii. My lost possessions returned, becoming relic alongside me. Blissful and brittle. Bent on stasis. In the midst of disintegrating form, where the end of a line begins the next. Expanding executions. Curtailing coda. *Will time tear down my Siberian stadium?* Rain reaches me as I reach for clouded sun. Last right of blessed debris. It's I that sees the dead one breathing. Death not just for anyone.

ID

Recover me lapse in plurals. Pauper umbilical floss and torch cranium. Trepidation body, lunge for your lack. I was starting to say, against need. Again gaining against. Pronouncing surgeries of parentheses. Light he craves. Contained contrasaid contrary. Pray, be provident. You are tallow where I am rendered. Was I so shadowing with your watch. The lapse is a mantis of my candlelight. Throwing shades. Never I was as athlete for longevity. Pelvis rituals and the such. Nay, I was extinguishing. Blazing betraying the still. Rhapsode of vaults and loss. Lapsing fleeing meltiful operations. I glister and dim when you happen, he. That is where we last left me. Spinning your sup empty drink. It wasn't the last where. We are everlast vanishing. Six minutes remaining five minutes behind. Lest you forget wax on the wane. Let it be that will do. The lapse is in the furthering of forgotten. Not know yet. His siege beat in evening. Bone weary. He improperly interpret me. Ay, I've had poor ed. It's not respite again. Not meaning once more. The skull I profit. Told time passes in the once. He its apostrophe. As soon as was not so precise after you possessed it. It was over it ended then. Then the end anew. Immoral imprecision. Welcome him to now is it. Moment wrench whens. A moment as old as it was. In my head I have a thought of moths drowned in pooling tissue. It is a fountain that rises from the weeds conveying the delicate flame, sourceless and injured. We wander most magnificent fields that way. Go ahead let it go. The fields are lawning from you. The lapse is the difference between them, yard and lea. Now and then I ought remind him of we. Good, this gets longer. I'm insiding. Cope just to make me so. Stoop down. Pluck white clovers awry. Now and then and then some I amass. But moltenly, moltenly. Mind was I so solution. Give way to clipped wings. You reap you till. Unsteady threads disarray the shorn. I'm lapsed in the copse. Somewhere you are I'm missing. Content in the expanse repeating our dissolve. Give me the span of diminishing. More will come, when he's decisively doused. The lapse is in the drowns. Friday night write. Dawning wrist. You need two hands for five and six. Where I am waterless sourceless clockless you watch. Drawing what warmth from figment flame I ask you. I ask you by tealight. From mine nothing you gain. I am everything he incisions. The streets is wilderness but there is no streets in the wilderness. That's you that's me stray. Leech of you like a bedsore. Gone lawn gone bed gone wisps ago. Still lots more. To work on. But a wick is patient where a glim is not. My wrist limping. Don't he see in the dark. The bathing moth belongs to us both. I was gypsied round the skull enjoying nature. The blues of locomotives whence meadows roared your lactose horizon. Shadows enjoin the massif. That's when I thrive the light. Blossom my little natural world. When he is nocturned and somnolent. Looking from his window. Worrying about aches. Tinkling his liquors away. So many bouquet sorrows. My head's on fire for your lantern, spinning silk. Mower of carbon mix metaphor dioxide. You decision I abide. To blend. The door to the shed creaks open. I know better by the sweet sweet lament of hinges. Every now and then a gust shuts it, being vulnerable to its structure. Entrails forming now. Black mourner's gown. Soul ascending smoke. The lapse is in voluptuous blaze. He worries, his length of worries. Cicadas mate. Their call is the boundary. He goes away I grow back. In spite of the scythe despite the stillness that permits the match. Hard for him, lit and sower person. Labored for I too harvested. Lapses a plot of distance. The mind crawls insectual evenings of waning moon. Tufts of grass conquer gloss. I might, I might, devoured by the light. I disobey the flame. Apologetically I would say. The horse tramples cerebrum pasture. You are cruel with the lash, it brings me to tears. I lick them as they rain before I rend. Good, this goes on. Lasting, lasting. It surges. I. Candle crop and lawn cannibal grazing. Your tractor blades make the most oppressive lines. I I I, I'm impressed. It was. It was from you I borrowed the motility of grids. I feel it six and natal. My death drive of a tractor. Fatal steed of thirst. Parts of the hide plunge to the earth. Earthmare. Lapse surfaces. His head begs the Plinian of me. But orderly, orderly. Once enough till it isn't, he. Who will be worsted. How about us both the worst of us both. Once enough because it once was. Settle ever. Mental settlements. Landminds. You cultivated my innocence. Forged it kneaded it. Relax. Relapse. Dying into you. Cache of hardened wax.

WHOSOEVER WE ARE

Sought so many sunrises into you so many cognitive floods. But what I seized became such artichoke pulp what I pried was because a hide. There was a fleece of light journeying gleans from the blade of my scythe a light to data mine for your rot motion of making visible. Sought so much in names the naming of whosoever we are to rise never nowhere in so flu luminous unripe bulbs of existence. There was a barn there was an oven they seeped heat and I saw us inside the fumes of gasoline where I've been the tanned thawed horizon. Sought the yard sought spent lawns in us whosoever we are product perceived drowned. Stood at points of made trace into sun out of appendage adjunct shadow. Dizzy look for me there trampling tilling troubling thistle mimesis doubling my grain store ex-erlebnis. There was edible supply I was murderous alive prior to bloom so many wrought rows of convict blossoms. Sought moth found votive candle where a kernel bud was the engine tic burrows fraught inside me wading neck deep empress fields. Mind or heart whosoever we are stood at the seat of thought the seat of feeling the entrance of ocean locution kitchens behind the putrefied perished peril eye. Constant beehive flight arrival to find or to plant presence never with reference to compass stifle the body betrayed. Immerse pulmonary memory at last there was honey there was trench there was silence at last whosoever we are dizzying insect. Sought the carcass shelter sought the mouth of a parched delta at last the compost path remark parchment at last the denied splendor of synapse blush.

PENINSULAE

Somewhere else and every elsewhere. All those elsewheres that
you were. Of some one else who was. Of whom I could not look.
Your profile is the peninsula. An invitation and rejection. Like
the obsession of waves for the coast. Or the harbor of an unex-
posed inland, besieged by tempests all the same. Xenonym scene
of aviary viewpoint and alert as much askance. No consoling
but in the temporary averted. You're in all your favorite places
to visit. To ponder and be pondered under flares. I would not
prove to be there. The awning of ache estates. But you would
not be forestalled. I am again sealed by the gander. Prosecuted
by my reproof, the curiosity of a glance. Meandered around your
features of projecting piers. Engaging the game of pretend. You
do not take notice of me. Your attention is fixed on how I am
to you. Askew and goldening your complexion. From a shadow
I read the notice. The doubt is in the say. Where else said I am.
Inner isthmus conflict hurling my cast. A history of collapse
when you return it. The look that interlinks us. Like the silhou-
ette of a lighthouse. Or the peaceful walk of the intervening
promontory, dividing a single continuous body into two names.
I am your chosen annex. The other half of you masked by a coy
intent to be seen. As some one else raging silence. The paene
of said profile. Periphery profile, almost ocean. Your scrutiny is
the strait. Between us mountainous terrain. The gap that does
more violence than the else you are. It's typhoon season in your
face ready to declare war. I am the invading flag caught against
the treacherous gale you wage. The silt that stains your violet

vacation shirt. The condensation at the bottom of your colada. Contemplating so contemptibly you stir nervously now. I'm stirring with you. Like the beached beast that I am. Or the interchanging posture you worm into, to seem slimmer at noon. Into parallel waters a fragile reflection stares back at a stranger. Where depths shake from my vantage something recognizable. I recognize the unstable countenance is mine. Upper cheek scar. Mongolian spot. Buddhist bun. Relic empire islets. Replica tidal flat. The island strands us. You've drunk your fill and I discern the flush. Emboldened I keep still the was of us long enough. I was the crane watching the light slide over you. Keeping calm in the undercurrent careful not to blink. I touch casually the blemishes that alarm me. See you mimic my movements to relish my remorse. But with my eyes I replace the mole from your chin to above the lashes. Sweep the sand from between your toes. You're as anxious as I by the suspect tenderness. The tickle it excites. We fall elsewhere away onto verges. I've become suddenly brave with my gaze. The play of make believe and hide-and-seek. I'm somewhere in the shallow end. An umbrella jostled from your drink and skirts across the jetty. Involuntarily vulnerable. We neither tumble after it. The undulation halts us. In the burlesque of beholding you disappear from me. Into renouncing crests restored. Back into the aversion of some else that I am. Slant and sight resin.

WILTED

I held the vase in my hands. I turned the vase over in my hands. I held the vase away from me. I held the vase out in front of me. I considered the vase. I considered how little I knew of the vase. How little of its origin. I will hold the vase a few moments longer. The moments are immemorial. I considered the vase might have once been a carafe but was no longer used so, for purposes I have not. I considered that I was a prism looking back at myself, misunderstanding the transparency. I considered that the surface of the vase was particle, the contents of the vase skeletal. I considered the contents of the vase were wilted. There was no bloom I could detect. The contents of the vase were wilting, the drought of a thousand thirsts. I held myself out in front of me narrowly reflecting. I held myself withered and blurred and uprooted earth. I held out in front of me scaffolding. I threw the vase through the window. Some things are throughout. From the impact a song was shouted. From whom did the song belong? I considered the collision. The wreckage created was a symphony. I like the sound of that. Notes were heard rung in each fragment of shattered glass falling and which fell to the floor. I called the notes shards. I titled the tune *Wilted*. One by one a melody of discordant shards settled into me. I studied the weeping tune as the shards made their home, so as to later remember all wrong which parts of the meter each once belonged. The shards belonged to me. More or less. In that nothing sung a most imperfect balance. I belonged to glass. I studied sounds strewn about. *Listen to what I have made,* I said to the window frame, *listen to what made me.* I listened for a little cry for life. I listened for a little cry of life. Listened so as to shatter so. I sighted first the shards together spread. I considered them notes of a larger ensemble searching for symmetry. I looked then through every shard separately. Every shard then looked through me. I handled them reflecting on origin, on consequence, on intentional fallacy. I handled each piece with delicacy. A song I was so easily wounded. I reassembled the notes in the likeness I wished always to see myself. Myself I had almost seen. Composed of crevices, of seams, always feeling my hands across embroidery. As I saw myself once upon the vase caked in soil, the vase once drunk from, flower petals fingering lightly the edges along my mouth. In the shards I searched for peace. In the music I sung for pieces. I tuned each edge of glass with my fingertips. There was no peace found. I turned again my attention to the window. I considered my likeness felt in the window. The cleft, the fissure I had left. I had put a hole through the window with the vase, making a supernova. I shattered the window with the vase for the song it would make, following me reflecting. I broke the vase and the window because I was no longer afraid. I did it because I was no longer afraid of a little shout of desperation. *I did it,* I announced to the remains, *because I was desperate for a song.* The silence made me desperate. I found keys instead. The keys were inaccurate, unsettling. The vase and the window, left as remains like that, were an indistinguishable rhapsody, each shard so hopelessly conducted. Each note so desperately considered. Out of tune. I looked for tarnishes. A light shone through the hole I left in the window, brightening banalities. The light left hues so as to interpret the cadence of shards, left as remains like that. I sung them together, the light and the glass, but had no means to solder them without imperiling myself. So I settled there on the floor. My eyes drew blood. I drew my eyes to lessen the light that was let in. I built the shards to form a vision that was teal and as of yet glaring. I built the shards to form a vision of myself that was let into spectacular hues. I gathered there in sea foam. I sat there as one life was extinguished and another one was renewed. I listened as the life renewed was as soon forgettable. On the floor I collected the shards into rows of tiny isles, less carefully with each pile, and orchestrated a mansion for myself. I opened the skin of my palms composing the façade, I drained my fingers into turquoise arias. Each shard cut a chorus I bled to restore myself. The soil, the music, the tune, the hues. The light, too, was less careful with its harmonies. Off-key with mine, it crescendoed a memorial body. I considered the orchestra. I settled into its pit. Now a day has passed. Several days have passed. A stanza of days has passed. A glass past. A day had past in glass. Some days have passed in glass. I like the sound of that. The frame of the window now supports a patchwork of iron and there will be no more flowers. Petals undetected still. The window, itself and the absent parts, are yet repaired. The window itself, missing members of itself, the window still lost of its quartets. I misremember the song. The light, now of a lesser intensity, divides the floor in half. The window is chlorophyll emitting absent energies, somber sounds. Sounds it let out into absent hues. The window wears a frame belonging to something else. The hole of it designed against its relation. The petals that I could not descry nor invent but whose evidence I loiter my voice for. I busy myself with the shards I had stored in the shadows before I slept. They will sing the dust. On one side of the floor, the side of lesser light, is a mist of constellations. On the other side of the floor, the side in which I had settled for sleep, are the shards in tiny likenesses I had bedded well bled. The mist myself miraged as brightly. I reconsider the glass I had gathered for sleep. I see myself in scales. The soil marks my crocodile skin. I consider some more the shards I had collected. The luster each part of me I have lacked, to let the notes last a little longer. I am a little longer desperate. Reflecting in the ruins, I get started on the activity of stacking. I stack the shards atop one another until gravity crumbles them. The dirt and dust cake the cuts on my fingers. I believed I was holding myself together. I thought I had drawn the music into myself. I believed the song of the shatter lasted me. Sung my throat to shreds. I dusted myself teal. I covered the shards with notes. I drew the fragments wrongly across me. What heat the light let in slowly intensified. A discomforting warmth moved across my pelt. I had slept under a bridge. The shade hides me from the light but warms the image, sheet music motions to shards. Until today. Until today as a consequence. Until today I woke. Today the floor has been swept, the window replaced. Something of myself like a metronome remains in the pyramids I once shaped. The violence remains. My hands, now bandaged, leave little beads of blood on their dressings. I beat them on the floor where the shards of me had once been. I consider me once been. Spread there like that, the wounds on my palms and fingertips pulsing in the dull sapphire. I take the form of a thing destroyed. The destruction of the window and vase returned to. I am unsure what to do with myself. I've lost much gathering. I've lost much in the gathering. I return to a shadow, to quit at last. I return to look once more for remains. Remains of blade, of whorls. To hunt for the hurt of collision. To gather the soot and dust and song I bleed to recover. Hurt hangs itself like a concerto. Hurt hangs itself like that, when the music is the trace of a bare linger. *Sing always farewell*, I said. So I consider home. I am home, I guess. I am home middest a litany that resists the oboes and violas of obliteration. Home is where collisions collect. I will score another song for my cruelties. For flower and thirst.

ROOM FROM WHICH WE ROSE

Brought forth fraught. Mere presence nearly absence. The room for whom rose. From rift. From scarlet phusis. Foolish for what is risen. Within a room sheltering what arises. No say and that were said stuffed in cupboards. Zero space to climb. But space enough for clambering descent. Prying. To be out of being. Red gerund stucco. The gaze dissonant perception. Chamber projecting stillness of said. Barely heard. Stilled in being unable. Rouge refusing aletheia. Seeped. Contained. Characteristics of the room. Angular anguish. Distraught center. All there is to say. Reciting roses. Planhs to thresholds. Faint world. Faint life. Abyss and viscera. Conversely held. Hazardous venture. The room a mind took as my own. Where say as trace. In such a world. Such a life. Such is strife. Arms folded across the kneecaps. Head resting on red. No room to lift it. Bald and no cap. Aching against the ceiling. Textualized body. Void composition. Stammering surface. From vibrations below. Letting go of rose recesses. Sputtering and daubing. Not decorating but defiling. Said stuffed in closets. The armoire noggin. In opposition to. Going nowhere but against. A frail attempt but still. Now head rests on right wall. Trying the hands limited as they are. Filing fingernails on the floor. The floor for whom rose cold. Carve. What is the idea. The idea is a lie. Leeway for my stay. Goes on this way. To witness and be witnessed. Bad blood of motion. Closed in. Perennial pose. The posture of folding into oneself. Opposite. Though not alone. Willed here to be gathered. Oppressed. Hearing but hardly. Hardly only thoughts. Hardly aware of why. For what purpose risen for. Only to return. To go nowhere and to realize there's nowhere to go. To know and not be able to say. The pain of saying. The pain of being apart. Away from whom but myself. Alone with his self. Drawing the withdraw. With little plasma clots. Beading then trickling down the legs. Making room for what little space pronounced. In the room which bounds. The heart pounds. For those moments ago. All for and by such toil. Lotus scoliosis. Guessed thought even mute. Suppose. Unfix my pose. But all unbearable. The failure from without. Desecrating the days. Between his legs. His leeway sway. Crude intrusion. Wound textures. Tumult blues. Timid rose emergence. Sink back within. Then those nights happen. The setting crimson. Raised contaminated. Nurtured fraught and forgotten. Until something giving way. Hear saws. From somewhere off. That somewhere near to me. A timbered tree. Chamber interjecting splinter of say which was. Rose felled effort. The ceiling sharpens arrows. Out of my head. From whom risen for. Verses. Ploughshares. Tilled lines of arthritic limbs. Compacted. Compost prose. Rose horizontal. Unquenchable pardon. Limn partition. Cellar civilian. Tile stare. Then steadying head on left wall. Taming the rose throbs. Refused sums. Neutral space. Lump inhabitance. Sawing his pillars. In the basement. Spelling my hymns. Chambers. Thoughts related to forests. Poorly voiced chorus. Of injured echoes. Rose torque. Forked tongue. In a metaleptic room he bends me. I bend into him. Agoraphobic claustrophobia. We live the room. The room lives me. Lifts him as I rise. To immediately meet its roof. Its walls. Its cupboards. Its closets. Envy. Envy of the albatross. Envy of embers. Envy to be what the room had risen. To be what the room has made me. But I'm his instead. Naked crude and crouched. Tree fallen from the rose in silence. A stump rising into the unheard dungeon. Greeted. Deleted. Eventual. Sustained. Caving in. Only room for folding rose.

WRAITH

Done gone. Was me. Spoken weres. Done gone and dug. First unearthed. Unthreaded. The form taken. By error. Textile. Little by little. Now myself. No self now. I'm remnants. Images away. Triumphant torture. Kept granules. Kept revenge. Grief keeping. Images cast. The ones that hadn't wandered. Too far. To some. Then to one. To someone else's gaze. Impacted. Sunk. Star strangled. The hands casting. Biddable shapes. Arrested and astray hands. Clutched. Worn grips. I had spoke. Speak you. Mostly the woes. Almost. The safest place for me was in the word. The words almost. The words I could not conjure. Couldn't place the names. For the life of me. Save for worst mine. Gumming words. In the grip of words. Always. Pursuing firmament. The ash blush of sun. I hadn't meant it then. Mean it now. It means now. Somewhere. Wearisome. Somewhere else. Into someone else. Somewhere else other than. Weary. For sustenance. Shelter alone. Pitch dark. Done gone. Voice your saw. The feeble see and witness. My carnation eyes. Teary scenes of rose. Volcano. Roam. Dissolve. Reformation. Go on. Regress. And I am saved. At last. For the worse. Worst pace of the wraith. Harmest event to write. To tear. Reprimand. Reminder. At a mindless clip. Reddened. I mean redone it. Entropic. Kaleidoscopic. Out of me lifing. Done. Gone. Done and gone. In. Without. In and out. In and out and on. I lifted the azure folds. Died. But for death I could not provide. Mornings come. Torturous dawns. Long after. Supplied incidents.

Indentured I did. As I was. Come back to insteads. Must be done. Resist. Mustn't be done. Couldn't become. Finishing. Gone done. Fowl words. All wrong. I hound the furthest skies. Bled best from parkway benches. After respite. It was probably. It is most likely. Counting steps. Before rest. Losing count. Counting steps in the other direction. Losing count again. Walking is how to lose it. After rest. Stay. See stoned and drunk flushed. Meandered in my head a bit. By some miracle returned to. The saw. When to I never want it. Pearl glares. Dizzy apparition. Somewhat. Sequestered. Sim fled. The we was because I was averse. To be nourished. You. Couldn't sustain you. Bloody stool. Skin tags. Rash. Heartburn heart murmur. Loyal to brands. The revolution and fast food. At what a pace. The devious sight of me. Disappearer. Too tiresome. Meandered I was. Throughout. Preposterous decades. Since lay. Since crawl. Since too helpless to move. Since bibs. Since the soiled briefs. The soiled briefs I hid. The soul that wets itself free. Such mortification. So much shame. Disgrace. Since the changing table. Since father's fists and ridicule. Since the witness. The witness who weaned me. Ever since. At the since. Since then. Impotent. Paradise haze. Unendurable figment. Inhabit. Torture habit. Since you. I remember you. Last in ache. Couldn't get to my feet. Familiar infancy. Seeing that. Said condemned. Addict said. Form of feeling. Can't place. Done gone. God dammit. Dead of night. Repeat. Return. Watches on. Paces. Cindering arch. Cindering museums. Mausoleum memories. To bits. The white walls. The crib. Still a child. But old enough. For bed. Tossed onto. Throwing fits. On the inside. Worse kind. Born in soul. Adopted adolescent body. Father red in the face. Always. Rough handled. A yelp. The welts. Receding witness. Not like this. Losing it. Lifted by the ankles. Swathed and spat on. Swift scream. The first rash. Likely. Probably. Lasting image. Ruins. Outlast. Sweaty crevices. Wiping. Wiping and more wiping. Then someone else's wipe. Required. Till the last days. Pristine between the legs. Always. Brief and lasting. Father's words. Absent father. Never known. I recreate him. I pace him. Imagined memories. The haven't. But felt. How could be. Remembered. Cast. Weres. Not words. Paced within four white walls. Your four white walls. Bequeathed. Like you paced. Father never stared you. Looked only where was darkened. Faint ring of dampness. For the briefs. Between bed and wall crevice. Whose relief. Their grief. Keeping. Vast. Various. In keeping. Feels same. Always. For some. A vision. Almost. Much all done. Couldn't control. The body. Let it go. Done gone. Most. Found again. In the footsteps. The cracks. See the opening. Crawls across the parkway. Vantage. The one. Father's. Yours. Few left to write. Some few. Same few. The room. The witness. Scarcely rearranged. Re-ing. Ring of urine. Ring of moon. Coming through. Unthreading. Couldn't help it. Like couldn't place. The seeping. Me porous imagining. Lasting anamnesis. Last remembrance. Failed image at last. Who am we but they. The pace I take. Rye. To summon father. To plead the witness. Mother. Indiscreet. With my screams. Goldening bedsheets. Briefs. Momentary gloamings. Bled into one. Not run into one. Squirm. From his rough hand. Clutches both ankles. To control. As I was. Controlled. I couldn't control. Borders. Horizons. Would. If could. If wanted. Not wanted. Since the wanting. Since withholding witness. Torture heritage transcendence. Beckon. The bench. The changing table. Rested. Changed. Done gone. Stalking sun. Suffocation stars. So many miles. In the pace. The march. In place. Outpace. Outplaced. Regression. Repress. Craving. Space to hide. Do go. The one. Not till now. Wasing and pacing. Recreations. Shun lifing. Elses. Everything. Nothing. To lose. All lost. Already. Almost already. Seep words. Nameless out of them. Won't see. Just the glisten. You. To the last. His child. Shame. Mortuary. Wrong. It's urns. Pace. Turn. Pace turn. About. Testify. The shouts. Burly father. Not. Anything he was. Someone else were. Endured. Fabric. Flesh. The word. The ward. Still. Except done. The endearing gone. Not so brawn. Kept the flaws. Kept partial. On hands and knees. Crawled to bed. They still happening. For wants. Needless. Need. Lessen. Deeds. Rough and stained. You. Last laid. Seen last laid. Since the first lay. Shame layers. Much shame. So it was. Except still is. Revisited. Gone and on. His open hand. Across the bottom. Red imprint. The gaze of witness. Same. Starry gaze. Mine. Socketed. Place to sit. At the gates. Desperate. To be done. Undone. You. So him. Must him. No father mustn't. Not the must of me. Urine musk. Shit musk. Stale. Stare. The pain. Stare the pain of musk away. Words. For the worst. Farewell. Worsening image. Seep imagine. Pace. Pasting. Not as vast. So vast. Belong to me not. Yours. Surviving him. Father. Seen. Through tears. Rose cheeks. Damn rose sun. Never wanted it. Again. A wonder. The without. The within. Within the without. Pain of see. The pain of say. Torturing. Intervening weres. Since crawl till cane. Father's. With the porcelain head. Tore across my skin. It rests now. Last by the bed. Tossed there. Cast down. Not like this. Not like his. Heritage. Fostered. Abandoned. Adopted. It's lost now. Soiled. Unearthed. Then wander since. Pace. Scrape. Pace. Scrape. The place. White walls. Outlet. Wet. Yelp. Welt. Shun. The farthest suns. The farthest rings. Furthering. Still furthering. Dried. Stained. But dying. Still death. Since. Instead. Supplied. Sore-eyed. Visions. Pounded and pulp. Incast skies.

From bench of overpass. Hazard. To pace. Upward. Always. Almost word. Father's name. Mine was. Matrimony. Witness. Name changed. Too many names. Not enough words for them. To place. Couldn't place accurate. That was you. That's the image. Wraith's lyric time. Possible. Laced my back. With cane. With fist. First fist. Then came cane. What's left. Fled. To someone else. To mend. Take in. I'm poured out. Fearsome. Swelled. Harped. Timorous. Torturous. You. Gut. Gums. Dug. Damp. Sun. Ash. Urn. Earth. Done gone weres. Formless keep. Myself. Little by little. I'm bits. By impact. To bit. Then to bits. To someone else's image. Speak him. Into place. Into my piece. Soiling briefs. Hazard conjuring. Sunken one. The else other than. Linen. Folding witness. It means now. Saved the unsafest scenes. Word dripping. As from inside the thighs. Between the legs. Hideout seem. No self now. It does not mean. Keeps going. Torrent drunk firmament. Except almost not. Always the almost. Pursuing different direction. Feeble vision voice. Return. To insteads. Since dark. Felt dark. Darkest sense. Blends. Rose bled. Father. Forgot. Unknown. As myself. Stranger. Before rest. Since lay. Afterward. The parkways. Last pace after. Last word estranged. First word same. Ever infant word. Meandered. To deny tortured mornings. To delay the name of dawn. Weary for pitch dark. The dark redone. For reddened sun. Out of me lifing. Failed life image. Control of it. Lost it. I couldn't. Ever so clutched. Wanting. But shunned. Stale stare. Stale stargaze. Star witness. Testify. On my behalf. From your bottom's crack. Hid. Above the legs. Held by ankles. Like a newborn. Half the self. Hate the self. Wiped for you. Lookout. Father's back. To swathe. To pace. Four white walls. Who are they but me. Desperately fled. But beckoned. Seeped. Crave. The outplace. Gleam of golden urns. Glinting. I am glare. Of one. Then some. Servant of someone else's vision. Was mine. Not mine. Never mine. Meandered a bit. In my mind. At a pace clip. Like since bibs. Goddammit. But the scream is swift. Other than meaning. Made up. Bed turned down. I turn about. Flee him. Flee you. Me fled. To be done. With cane keeping the pace. Torrent pain of say. First remembrance. Almost. Last murmur. Always. Looked for the place. Looked down. Nowhere safe on the eyes. My optic bouquets. Died. Still death. Saw red. In father's face. Red relief. Will keep the grief. Seeing that. Intact. The white walls. Around him. Witness. Releasing up the sheets. Save for worst yours. Peeling urine. Off the white walls. Volcano ash. Always ever must. Last rashes. Furthest evers. Wraith disgrace. Shame soul. Father. The rough embers. Uncontrolled kaleidoscope. Insiding. Folding inward. Last after the rye. Harmest event to write. Gone. Done.

WRITHE

I wanted. I tried. I attempted. I tired. A feverish temperature came over me. I tired of temptation. I wanted to try. Swore I would. I believed I had done so. For some time. Hollowing the while. Toiling seasons. But really, I couldn't. Until I realized. Fuck. Sworn some a second time. Swear I won't repeat it. Shit. I've been afflicted. I was tempered down. A dull bulb. Okay. Say. I tried. I tried to want. I tried to want to. I tried to want to write you. I tried to want to write you epistles into the skin. But I am infinitive. Why not? Why not. Yes. That's it. To not. Not to be shielded. There it was. There's the writhe for which I longed. I loved once was. Then she was gone and toil persisted. What's the harm. Too many harms. A harm too many. Yes yes. I knew I did not know. Yet for certain. To surmise. That was me with a sharp cry. On the inside. Taming a tendon. Here and there. That one, then the next. The nights spent on anatomical caresses. They were all bastille. Next I gave just a gentle shove. I had not desired to. It happened and then it happened. Pressing with what timid might left onto ligaments. The finest leather. Light and amber. I ground my incisors. Stained my mouth a hide. The loving mood gave way. Apprehension has its violences, too. And that as to laughter. In them I seethed so colossal. Now I receive presents. They're the bauble kind. Precious only to those who gift them. I can't recall. I accepted them exasperated and not without impatience. There were other gratuities I wanted nothing to do with. Documents, certificates. Proof of some kind or other. They were pieces of sandpaper. To whittle the daily grind supine. The days were given to an impending signature. For god's sake those parchments. When he's ready, when he's ready. When the patient's gathered enough strength. Where's the anesthetic. They wanted me mollusk. A sigil was always anticipated. I'll give them that. Then I could expire, my affairs in order. They'd get them out of me. Sooner or later. Craven as I am, heinously if they must. Soon I was. Was it will be. Soon, soon. I'd prefer their forgery. Carve my name onto my grave. But whatever you do don't keep it lush. Keep it dust. I kept them waiting but wanted them gone. They tried me. I was roughed up. But well before, well before. The joke's on them. No fun for anyone. I was promised there'd be a vigil. They wanted me a wake. I want of none. All those embers. Give me tears instead. Has it been that long? It's been a beach ago. Beach glass, was it? No, it wasn't. Guess we'll go there, then. No, not there. That's where I'd dreamt of going. So long, there I am. Torrid with the sunrise. I was limp anyway. A limpet. To thrash. At never have been so smooth. Ever so amethyst. Regardless I tended to my collection of little runaways. To be so metamorphic. That's the hospital-bed dream. They were suspicious. I was shore of it this time. Can't fault them. I had my suspicions too. I adhered as far as any scallop goes to disturbances. Those wind and wave conditions. When. When the tumult kept me living. Thrive of ebb and flow. I was in the profession of erosion. The falls of wearing out. Summers of a fine thaw. Featureless of letters on a page. Won't go back can't go back. I can get with that. If I'm up for it. Though never was. I lost the limber of the wrist clutching blankets too tight. So it seems. But enough. Quite! Enough with analogies. Enough anatomy. Enough of anemone.

Just this once just to be. Quietly, quietly. That would be justice served. A day hard earned. Paid in their accumulation. Why? When I begged instances. Today I woke to crows outside my window. There were more of them than usual. They were more chipper. Their vocalizing more-than-usual even stopped tourists on the street. It was uplifting. I have caws for that. Next I awoke not to my surprise being tended. What a strange reversal of fortune. I squirmed. I was a state of squandering. Never cared for the attention. I have only misfortune to speak. Okay. I'm going into the water. They restrained me. Said father's not here. But you'll see him soon, soon. It's shallow breathing. The same gurney. Gasp gasp gasp. I'm deadly alive to the tune of my lips all atremble. The air just seeps out of me. The upper lip lifts and ripples while the lower lip curls. Coos and awwing. Like the infant writer. What a poor bebe. I was asemic. No. Anemic was it? Pardon the prognosis. Forgive my wrongdoing. Pat my head dry my chin. They wanted me tame. Reading books all through life. I gave awry interpretations, often misquoted. Hehe. I tried rather for dishonorable deeds. Drawn a will of intangible possessions. I possessed hardly words. Their loss the same as mine. See what that buys them. I've had enough. Leave me your assets! I said it's getting brighter. The chokes claim what I said to say the least. They only heard a compliment. Ha! I grasped for the brightness but got indifferent hands. Go where it's brightest, dear. They didn't know. But that's what they said. They were full of ideas and had no idea. I didn't know. In spite of it all I could always take comfort in their failing me. At least there was that. Such sweet strokes though. I knew them not tenderly. How ever. I tried. Ever did I try. Benefit of doubt. It must be. I tried for so many instants of gulfs. Made attempts at a murmur. They bloated me and now I'm diminished. They'll learn. I don't satisfy easily. When I wanted fallen. They want me felled away. Evening was coming. Eve will come. Or I to she. Eventually. Or not. She shimmered near to me. In forests on coasts. I had my doubts. Troubled breath for surety. Eve was uncertain. Therein lied my love. Of her shimmers. Ever after. Relentless afterwards. An end, the end is coming. Persist. They said swallow. I awoke again to their herd. Strange to see them soar like that. Like parting handkerchiefs for the hazardous passage. Swallows in uncertain circles. With seizure in their sway. Suddenly. All of a sudden. Oh so sudden. The saliva had sweetened the corner of her mouth. A sign. Impossible to communicate. The taste of aluminum and rust had abated. Still they were aggrieved. In the evening they had had enough. They fetched pillows, raised the top portion of the bed for a posture more properly suited to write. Words had to do and I was the worst for them. Of a sudden I saw. What they saw. What I tired to see. I was. I waited too. I waited with them. Her head craned. They hoped to find at last no heaving of the chest. Her mouth parted. Hadn't shut. It fitted me. The increasing distance between the pants. Eve had taken my place. I let a cry. Get me out of here! Take me to the boardwalk. It was light but gaining brightness. I was beginning. I wanted. I bided. I didn't try.

TEAR

Light wishes inwardly, lunatic illuminations.

Must wild wept, with the mad ones in my wilderness mouth.

Famished, laid rustling, the match answered elsewhere.

Chord of morning timbre offers calm becoming.

Stark nervous sky, supine stabbing, and my end.

Mount lashes, where getting away means synthetic sigh.

Fit moments hid, bent to forget, the whip of utterance craves dust.

Undone, unsound, now the trembling crescendo.

Language, the somber arena, conjuncture of iteration.

Caught before the word, caught after it said, tooth conduit of charged illiteracy.

Angry, that of me, the centurion objectivity.

This world, tolerating me, shattered is.

Short-lived with fragments, sighing visions of unwell sorrow.

Thought or the burning, open bright the sulfur, keep speech in fatal intimacy.

The mountain slides, yokes the valley below, nourishes the unsteady treaty.

Madly alive, shouting help to the sky, delusively softly.

Mass wasting spoke sedimentary condolences, blistered stone in my bones.

The cruelty of plots, betraying deeper gardens, tenor of the brink.

Teething every trace, enraptured interiors.

I was the hallucination once, secludedness, riposting the iris.

Voyaging my tongue toward silence.

The contention of yonderly coordinates, coming to what has been.

To thaw twin fever of paradox, to noose truth, in rocking play.

Suddenly, ever, remembrance's saying, inferable rock paths to heart of breach.

The landslide mind, a concealment and clearing of sod beyond.

Fire's voyeur naps in the shade, dreaming away the cavernous blister.

Annulled identity, the fever pitch of treble clef, prior tone of fuck massacres.

An ontology of indecision commands rhythm.

Notations of emptiness, the there is that remains outside being.

Field of vision, a fraudulent promise of horizons, of penetrable distance.

To crave contact ridicules the tundra within.

The timpani tears in me.

The gash that beats the waterfall into a river, this head that is hospice.

A singular tear, to restore the residue of a previous murmur, nearness apart.

Smooth traps of memory, zenith, burst without.

Thought that does not belong to it.

Turn into quiet circularity, before and after collapse.

Dig, you'll not reach me.

Breathe, precede and exceed, in between appears the apparition.

Respiration of shadow, pulsing the duress.

The twilight threshold.

The inner rift extinguished.

Staccato soul.

Commence immense death.

Continue deaf into eternity.

Please forgive everything about me.

Notes

ASUNDER

. . . to forget that life is death's prisoner. Emil Cioran, "On Death" (trans. Ilinca Zarifopol-Johnston).

. . . tomorrow will always be late in arriving. Ghérasim Luca, "The Inventor of Love" (trans. Julian and Laura Semilian).

I breathe you / day and night I breathe you [. . .] *you seal you fascinate them / you cover me / I discover you I invent you / sometimes you deliver yourself* [. . .] *I write you / you think me.* Luca, "The End of the World: To Embody" (trans. Mary Ann Caws).

". . . the portrait of Jacqueline." Dora Maar, "Jacqueline Lamba with arrow."

". . . the baboon in the witch's kitchen." Goethe's *Faust*.

". . . Masson's Vitruvian man." André Masson, *Acéphale*.

". . . Ortega's garden." José Ortega y Gasset, "The Dehumanization of Art."

SOON TO BE

. . . the name of the bow is life, but its work is death. Heraclitus, *Fragments*.

THE ANIMAL OF EXISTENCE

. . . I preferred the sharpest corner of this room to be alone in. Pierre Reverdy, "Always Alone" (trans. Ron Padgett).

. . . forget me, know me not, yes, that would be the wisest, none better able than he. Samuel Beckett, "Text IV" (trans. author).

. . . one word is not enough to save the rest. Philippe Sollers, *The Park* (trans. A. M. Sheridan Smith).

YEARNS
". . . Pig Cupid." Mina Loy, "Love Songs."

WANDERLUST
". . . the sad bed of the oriole's song." René Char, "The Oriole" (trans. Mary Ann Caws).

". . . the conductor's wand in the underbrush." Baudelaire, "The Thyrsus" (trans. Louise Varèse).

IN MEDIAS RES
". . . my little Moscas around me." Ben Jonson, *Volpone.*

WHOSOEVER WE ARE
Title inspired by Rilke's "Initiation."

Acknowledgments

Tremendous gratitude to John Yau and everyone at Black Square Editions for ushering *The Animal* into existence, and to Austin Carder at *Caesura*, Laura Vena at *Entropy*, Douglas Glover at *Numéro Cinq*, Garett Strickland at *PLINTH*, and Gabriel Blackwell at *The Rupture*, for giving several of these texts an initial home.

To first readers Carlos Lara and Sawako Nakayasu, for their brilliance, attention, and generosity.

To Christine Shan Shan Hou, for dressing *The Animal* in their hypothetical arrangements, and Shanna Compton, for shaping it into a domesticated object.

To Miriam Atkin, Josh Barber, Tom Carlson, Billie Chernicoff, Iris Cushing, Pam Dick, Forrest Gander, Rainer Hanshe, Brenda Iijima, Sharon Israel, Anton Ivanov, Jonathan Larson, David Lau, Eugene Lim, Anna Moschovakis, Vi Khi Nao, Steven Seidenberg, Sam Truitt, Derek White, and Rachael Wilson, for their kinship and encouraging support.

To Wayne Koestenbaum, Mary Ann Caws, and John Brenkman, for their nurturing wisdom, sustaining mentorship, and gifts of conversation.

To André Aciman, Donald Breckenridge, Ritch Calvin, John Davis, Nico Israel, Richard Kaye, Marina Perezagua, and Ayesha Ramachandran, for steering me back to previously abandoned paths.

To my family and friends near, far, and gone, for their inexhaustible patience, everlasting influence, and camaraderie in drink.

And forever and always to Erin Fleming, whose love continues to make palpable undreamt immensities, and to whom my fear of death is indebted.

About the Author

Jared Daniel Fagen is a Korean-American writer. His prose poems, essays, and conversations have appeared in *The Brooklyn Rail*, *Fence*, *Lana Turner*, and *Asymptote*, among other publications. He is the editor and publisher of Black Sun Lit, a PhD candidate in Comparative Literature at the CUNY Graduate Center, and an adjunct lecturer at the City College of New York. Born in Jeollanam-do, he lives in Brooklyn and the western Catskills. *The Animal of Existence* is his first book.

Black Square Editions was started in 1999 with the intention of publishing translations of little-known books by well-known poets and fiction writers, as well as the work of emerging and established authors. After twenty-three years, we are still proceeding book by book.

Black Square Editions—a subsidiary of Off the Park Press, Inc, a tax-exempt (501c3) nonprofit organization—would like to thank the following for their support.

Tim Barry
Robert Bunker
Catherine Kehoe
Taylor Moore
Goldman Sachs
Pittsburgh Foundation Grant
Miles McEnery Gallery (New York, New York)
I.M. of Emily Mason & Wolf Kahn
Galerie Lelong & Co. (Paris, France)
Bernard Jacobson Gallery (London, England)
Saturnalia Books
& Anonymous Donors

Black Square Editions

Richard Anders *The Footprints of One Who Has Not Stepped Forth* (trans. Andrew Joron)

Andrea Applebee *Aletheia*

Eve Aschheim and Chris Daubert *Episodes with Wayne Thiebaud: Interviews*

Eve Aschheim *Eve Aschheim: Recent Work*

Anselm Berrigan *Pregrets*

Garrett Caples *The Garrett Caples Reader*

Billie Chernicoff *Minor Secrets*

Marcel Cohen *Walls (Anamneses)* (trans. Brian Evenson and Joanna Howard)

Lynn Crawford *Fortification Resort*

Lynn Crawford *Simply Separate People, Two*

Thomas Devaney *You Are the Battery*

Ming Di (Editor) *New Poetry from China: 1917–2017* (trans. various)

Joseph Donahue *Infinite Criteria*

Joseph Donahue *Red Flash on a Black Field*

Rachel Blau DuPlessis *Late Work*

Marcella Durand *To husband is to tender*

Rosalyn Drexler *To Smithereens*

Brian Evenson *Dark Property*

Jared Daniel Fagen *The Animal of Existence*

Serge Fauchereau *Complete Fiction* (trans. John Ashbery and Ron Padgett)

Jean Frémon *Painting* (trans. Brian Evenson)

Jean Frémon *The Paradoxes of Robert Ryman* (trans. Brian Evenson)

Vicente Gerbasi *The Portable Gerbasi* (trans. Guillermo Parra)

Ludwig Hohl *Ascent* (trans. Donna Stonecipher)

Isabelle Baladine Howald *phantomb* (trans. Eléna Rivera)

Philippe Jaccottet *Ponge, Pastures, Prairies* (trans. John Taylor)

Ann Jäderlund *Which once had been meadow* (trans. Johannes Göransson)

Franck André Jamme *Extracts from the Life of a Beetle* (trans. Michael Tweed)

Franck André Jamme *Another Silent Attack* (trans. Michael Tweed)

Franck André Jamme *The Recitation of Forgetting* (trans. John Ashbery)

Andrew Joron *Fathom*

Andrew Joron *Oo*

Karl Larsson *FORM/FORCE* (trans. Jennifer Hayashida)

Hervé Le Tellier *Atlas Inutilis* (trans. Cole Swensen)

Eugene Lim *The Strangers*

Michael Leong *Cutting Time with a Knife*

Michael Leong *Words on Edge*

Gary Lutz *I Looked Alive*

Michèle Métail *Earth's Horizons: Panorama* (trans. Marcella Durand)

Michèle Métail *Identikits* (trans. Philip Terry)

Albert Mobilio *Me with Animal Towering*

Albert Mobilio *Touch Wood*

Albert Mobilio *Games & Stunts*

Albert Mobilio *Same Faces*

Pascalle Monnier *Bayart* (trans. Cole Swensen)

Christopher Nealon *The Joyous Age*

María Negroni *Berlin Interlude* (trans. Michelle Gil-Montero)

Doug Nufer *Never Again*

John Olson *Echo Regime*

John Olson *Free Stream Velocity*

Eva Kristina Olsson *The Angelgreen Sacrament* (trans. Johannes Göransson)

Juan Sánchez Peláez *Air on the Air: Selected Poems* (trans. Guillermo Parra)

Véronique Pittolo *Hero* (trans. Laura Mullen)

Pierre Reverdy *Prose Poems* (trans. Ron Padgett)

Pierre Reverdy *Haunted House* (trans. John Ashbery)

Pierre Reverdy *The Song of the Dead* (trans. Dan Bellm)

Pierre Reverdy *Georges Braque: A Methodical Adventure* (trans. Andrew Joron and Rose Vekony)

Valérie-Catherine Richez *THIS NOWHERE WHERE*

Barry Schwabsky *Book Left Open in the Rain*

Barry Schwabsky *Feelings of And*

Barry Schwabsky *Heretics of Language*

Barry Schwabsky *Trembling Hand Equilibrium*

Jeremy Sigler *Crackpot*

Jørn H. Sværen *Queen of England* (trans. Jørn H. Sværen)

Genya Turovskaya *The Breathing Body of This Thought*

Matvei Yankelevich *Some Worlds for Dr. Vogt*